ROLE PLAYING
THE PRINCIPLES OF SELLING
Second Edition

David Sellars III
Davenport College

SOUTH-WESTERN

THOMSON LEARNING ™

Australia • Canada • Mexico • Singapore • Spain • United Kingdom • United States

SOUTH-WESTERN
THOMSON LEARNING

Acquisitions Editor: Rob Zwettler
Project Editor: Kelly Spiller
Art and Design Supervisor: Annette Spadoni
Permissions Editor: Doris Milligan

Production Manager: Bob Lange
Director of EDP: Jane Perkins
Printer: R.R. Donnelley, Crawfordsville

NOTE: Actual brand names are used throughout this text. "Fusion," "HydroFlow," and "Propulsion Plate System" are registered trademarks of Brooks Shoes, Inc., a subsidiary of Wolverine World Wide, Inc. "Nike 180 Air" and "Nike Air Max" are registered trademarks of Nike, Inc." "Reebok ERS" is a registered trademark of Reebok, Inc.

Printed in the United States of America
1 2 3 4 5 6 7 13 12

For more information about our products, contact us at:
Thomson Learning Academic Resource Center
1-800-423-0563

For permission to use material from this text, contact us by:
Phone: 1-800-730-2214
Fax: 1-800-730-2215
Web: http://www.thomsonrights.com

Library of Congress Catalog Card Number: 91-28292

ISBN: 0-03-055382-2

Asia
Thomson Learning
60 Albert Street, #15-01
Albert Complex
Singapore 189969

Australia
Nelson Thomson Learning
102 Dodds Street
South Melbourne, Victoria 3205
Australia

Canada
Nelson Thomson Learning
1120 Birchmount Road
Toronto, Ontario M1K 5G4
Canada

Europe/Middle East/Africa
Thomson Learning
Berkshire House
168-173 High Holborn
London WC1 V7AA
United Kingdom

Latin America
Thomson Learning
Seneca, 53
Colonia Polanco
11560 Mexico D.F.
Mexico

Spain
Paraninfo Thomson Learning
Calle/Magallanes, 25
28015 Madrid, Spain

I wish to dedicate this book to my wife, Janie, and to my children, Brooke and Nate.

PREFACE

Goals of the First Edition

The first edition of *Role Playing the Principles of Selling (RPPS)* was the result of a very unfortunate personal experience. Although I studied marketing for six years in college and even took a course in selling, my first few months as a sales representative for the Pillsbury Company were disastrous. College had not adequately prepared me for a career in sales. It was only by trial and error that I became successful.

When I accepted a teaching position at Davenport College, I searched for a text that would teach my students the sales presentation skills I considered so necessary. None existed, so I developed my own text, which would achieve the following goals:

1. Adapt proven sales presentation and training techniques used in industry to a college selling course.

2. Provide a means for students to build their own sales presentations, using a simple, step-by-step, programmed-learning process, which would ensure that the concepts were applied in the recommended manner.

3. Provide an opportunity for students to learn by doing and to practice sales techniques using extensive role playing exercises.

4. Involve students in evaluating sales presentations to help reinforce the concepts in the text.

I am very happy to report that the first edition has been a big success. Over 150 colleges and universities have adopted *RPPS*. Thousands of students throughout the United States and Canada have developed sales presentations using the principles in the text. Approximately 1,200 traditional and non-traditional-aged students have completed evaluations of *RPPS* and have given it very high ratings. Ninety-five percent said it helped them develop an effective presentation, and 90 percent agreed it was worth the money they paid for it. Most of the professors who adopted *RPPS* were also very enthusiastic about how it enhanced the skill-development process.

Improvements for the Second Edition

The main features that have helped make the first edition so successful have not been changed. However, my experience as a marketing manager has taught me that one must constantly improve a product for it to stay ahead of competition and meet the needs of a changing marketplace. While many textbook revisions reflect only cosmetic changes, over 80 percent of the first edition of *RPPS* has been revised and updated. The numerous improvements have been made in response to suggestions from adopters, reviewers, and students. The following is a list of some of these improvements.

1. A continuing case study has been provided, which features the development of a sales presentation for a product students can relate to—running shoes. Students will follow Jeff Dykehouse, a recently hired sales representative,

as he explores the selling process for Fusion running shoes. Students will experience the challenge of building a sales presentation and the excitement of closing a sale—from gathering information for the presentation to prospecting and qualifying, and from calling the athletic shoe buyer for an appointment to conducting the presentation and closing the sale.

2. All of the examples in the text are new. More examples for selling services are included so that product and service selling now are given equal treatment.

3. A chapter on using the telephone to get appointments has been added. Students can develop and role play the telephone call.

4. Sections on the preapproach, questioning, and active listening have been expanded.

5. A section has been added to clarify the differences among features, advantages, and benefits. Numerous examples are provided to illustrate how a product or service's features and benefits must be matched up with the prospect's problems and needs.

6. Developing good customer relations through follow-up and service is explained in a new section.

7. The process of developing and role playing a sales presentation has been simplified, while the effectiveness of the presentation has been elevated.

8. The wholesale price of the text has been reduced to make it more affordable to students.

Organization

The text begins with an overview of the process of developing a sales presentation and an explanation of the use of role playing to learn how to sell. A section called "Overcoming Fear" is included in Chapter 1 to help students deal with the apprehensions of role playing in class. Examples of products and services that students might select for their projects are provided in Chapter 2. Chapter 3, called "Acquiring Background Information," not only details the information needed for the presentation but explains where to obtain it. Prospecting, securing an appointment, and determining the sales call objective are all discussed in Chapter 4.

The main focus of *RPPS* is in Chapters 5 through 8, which detail the four parts of an effective sales presentation: Approach, Securing Desire, Handling Objections, and Closing the Sale. Each of these chapters contains an explanation of the steps in the sales presentation and a complete salesperson–prospect dialogue to show how these steps would be used to sell Fusion running shoes. Planning Guides are included in each section so students can apply the steps to their product or service in the recommended manner.

At the end of these four chapters, students are given detailed instructions on how to role play the steps. The professor can have students role play the Approach, Securing Desire, Handling Objections, and Closing the Sale sections in addition to the complete presentation. If the professor feels there is not enough time to role play each part in class, students can role play them on their own, since no lecture is required. In this way, students will be better prepared to role play the complete presentation at the end of the semester. Rating forms are provided for each of the four parts and for the complete presentation.

Teaching Aids

A comprehensive *Instructor's Manual*, which includes a test bank and transparency masters, is available to professors who adopt *RPPS*. It contains detailed instructions on how to use role playing to teach the principles of selling. Lesson plans are provided for extensive, moderate, limited, and minimal use of role playing in class, so professors can choose the amount of role playing that is appropriate for their course objectives. An audiotape of actual student role plays, which illustrates how the steps are applied, is provided with the manual. The videotape of student role plays, which was produced for the first edition, is available to new adopters. Details of how to obtain the videotape are in the *Instructor's Manual*.

The National Center for Experiential Sales Training offers award certificates to the student in each class who the professor believes did the best job developing and role playing the presentation. Details of this program are in the *Instructor's Manual*. This is the most complete and comprehensive training system that has ever been developed for a college- or university-level course in selling.

Acknowledgments

I would like to thank all the sales representatives, sales managers, sales trainers, and students I have worked with over the years who have added to my knowledge of selling. I would also like to thank the professors who reviewed the manuscript of the second edition and were willing to share their ideas on how to improve this text: Mary Anderson (Frostburg State College), Robert E. Batson (University of Hartford), Marilyn Lewis (Abilene Christian University), Lou Mansfield (Kankakee Community College), John A. Mauch (American Institute of Business), John Montgomery (Ferris State University), Lavern Pich (Mohawk College), Musa Pinar (Saint Joseph's College), John Robbins (Winthrop College), Joan R. Weiss (Bucks County Community College), and Lawrence E. Wharton (Mt. Hood Community College).

I would especially like to acknowledge the people who helped develop the continuing case study, which features the Fusion running shoe. Jeff Dykehouse, a former student of mine, used Fusion for his project. Much of the information in the text related to Fusion is his. Jeff did an incredible job with his presentation and will be a very successful businessman someday. I am very grateful to Bob Sorensen, Director of Product Line Development, and Jeff Costello, Regional Account Executive, at Brooks Shoe, Inc., a subsidiary of Wolverine World Wide, Inc., for their time and help in developing the case. Their efforts will make a significant contribution to the training of thousands of future sales representatives.

Several members of The Dryden Press staff deserve recognition. Rob Zwettler, senior marketing editor, saw the potential for *Role Playing the Principles of Selling* back in 1986. A former salesperson himself, he recognized that this text filled a gap in the preparation of college students for a career in sales. I would also like to thank Kelly Spiller, project editor, for guiding the text through the steps of production; Annette Spadoni, designer; and Maureen Duffy, copy editor.

Finally, I would be remiss if I did not thank Penny Taylor and Heidi Malski for typing the manuscript. Somehow, they managed to learn how to read my writing and to meet all of my deadlines.

David Sellars III
November 1991

CONTENTS

OVERVIEW

Learning Objectives

The goal of *Role Playing the Principles of Selling (RPPS)* is to teach you how to sell. You will be provided with an opportunity

1. to learn the steps in an effective sales presentation,
2. to apply the steps to a real-world situation,
3. to develop persuasive communication skills, and
4. to build your self-confidence.

Training Method

Selling is a skill and, like any skill, you have to actively do it to learn it. Can you imagine trying to learn how to type by just reading about it? It is impossible. This is true of selling, too. To learn how to sell, you must experience it. The best training method short of structured on-the-job experience is role playing. You will learn how to sell by using this technique, which is used extensively in industry to train sales representatives.

You will develop a complete sales presentation on a product or service you select and role play it with your professor or another student acting as a prospect. You will assume the position of a field sales representative for a manufacturer, wholesaler, service operator, or another company. You are not to assume the position of a salesperson working in a retail store. Field (outside) selling was chosen because it provides more of a challenge and offers a potential for high income and advancement.

The type of presentation approach you will use is called *need satisfaction selling*. It involves asking questions during the presentation to find out the problems and needs of the prospect, then providing benefits and features of your product or service that will solve the problems or satisfy the needs. Need satisfaction selling is the approach most business firms use.

How You Will Benefit

The benefits to using *RPPS* are extensive. First, role playing will allow you to apply the concepts discussed in this course to a real-world situation. You will learn and retain more than you would without role playing—and this class will be fun. Second, the step-by-step approach and extensive use of examples in this training manual will better prepare you for role playing. Research conducted by the National Center for Experiential Sales Training has shown that students who used *RPPS* are able to deliver a more effective presentation and thus earn higher grades on their presentations than students who did not. Third, it will take less time to develop a sales presentation because of the detailed, "how to," step-by-step instructions provided. Finally, you will be much better prepared to pursue a high-paying career in sales if you so choose.

Overcoming Fear

Most students, when they learn they are going to be involved in role playing, become very apprehensive. Their fears are a result of the fact that they know nothing about developing a sales presentation and have never experienced role playing.

Fear is a natural reaction to encounters that are new to us. A certain amount of nervousness under these conditions is good, just as it is in selling. If your adrenaline is going, you are able to think and react more quickly. The key to managing fear is to let it work for you, not against you.

There are three ways to overcome excessive fear and to build self-confidence. First, you must understand how fear is created. Most people think encountering people or the environment causes fear. This is not true. It is the way *you choose* to react to people and your environment that causes fear. The first time you got up to give a speech or an oral report in class you probably experienced a lot of fear, yet another student took it in stride. Both of you were speaking to the same people in the same room. The students were receptive and wanted you to do a good job. So it was not the students who caused the fear, it was you. If it was the students, even your professor would be nervous during a class lecture. When you experience fear and anxiety while role playing or preparing to role play, be aware of your fear and say to yourself over and over again, "Do I want to make myself feel this way?" Remember, your professor and fellow students support you and want you to do a good job.

The second way to overcome fear is to be thoroughly prepared to role play. That's where this text will help. It provides detailed instructions on how to prepare your presentation and role play it. There will be no question in your mind about what you should say and do during a role-playing exercise. If you follow the instructions and properly prepare, you will build your self-confidence and you will not be overwhelmed by fear.

Finally, fear can be overcome through experience. *RPPS* will provide you with numerous opportunities to role play your presentation either alone or with other students. Try not to be too concerned with fear. When you feel yourself getting uptight about role playing, reread this section. It should help. Also consider talking to your professor about it.

Steps in the Selling Process

The steps in the selling process you will be studying this semester are provided next. While *RPPS* focuses on the steps *during* the sales presentation, the other steps are provided here so you understand that the presentation is only a portion of a sales representative's job.

A unique feature of this text is the use of a continuing case study. All of the following steps will be applied to an actual company and product. You will see how Jeff Dykehouse developed a sales presentation for Brooks Shoe, Inc., a subsidiary of Wolverine World Wide, Inc. He sells the Fusion running shoe to Penny Taylor, a buyer at a sporting goods store.

Prior to the Sales Presentation

Step 1. Acquire information on your industry, company, product or service, and competition

Step 2. Develop a list of prospects and acquire information about them

Step 3. Qualify your prospects

Step 4. Contact prospects and make appointments

Step 5. Develop a profile and determine your sales call objective for each prospect

Step 6. Develop your presentation

Step 7. Develop an efficient route through your territory

Step 8. Introduce yourself to the receptionist or secretary and ask to see the decision maker

During the Sales Presentation

Step 9. Open your presentation with the decision maker (the Approach)

Step 10. Secure desire for your product or service

Step 11. Handle objections

Step 12. Close the sale

After the Sales Presentation

Step 13. Update prospect and customer records

Step 14. Build customer relations through follow-up and service

On the inside front cover of *RPPS* is a guide called "Steps in a Sales Presentation." It summarizes the steps in each of the four sections of a presentation. You should refer to it when you are preparing to role play.

CHOOSING A PRODUCT OR SERVICE

Choosing a product or service for your sales presentation is the first step toward accomplishing the goals of this project. You should choose one in which you have interest and ready access to information.

If you enjoy skiing, you could sell a brand of skis to a sporting goods store. If you are a stereo enthusiast, you could sell the model you own to a stereo shop. Perhaps you like clothes. Selling a line of jeans to a clothing retailer would be an excellent choice.

You may wish to choose a product or service that is related to your future career. If you are an advertising major, you could sell radio or television time to a retailer. If you are planning a career in retailing, you could sell a cash register to a buyer for a chain of retail stores. If transportation and distribution are career areas you are considering, selling a truck leasing program to a manufacturer would help prepare you. Whatever you choose, it should be something about which you can get excited. Enthusiasm is an important element of a successful presentation. If you are not excited about what you are selling, you cannot expect your prospect to be excited about it and want to buy it.

To be prepared for your presentation, you must have a thorough knowledge of the industry, and specifically the product or service you are selling, the company you are selling for, the company and person you are selling to, and the major competitors in your field. This necessitates having access to information in these areas. *Ideally, the information should be available locally.* If you choose a product or service that is marketed nationally, and the firm is not located in your area, you may not be able to get the information you need in time to meet the deadlines for this project. If the firm is not located in your area, information about its products may be available from a distributor, sales representative, or retailer near you.

You may have a parent, relative, friend, or neighbor who is actively involved in sales. Selecting their product would ensure access to the information you need. Perhaps you work for a company that has a product you could sell. This would also be a good choice. Make sure your selection is currently being marketed. Sufficient background information will not be available for a hypothetical product or service. You can always check the Yellow Pages for ideas. Your local chamber of commerce could be helpful too.

If you are selling for a manufacturer or distributor with a line of products, it is generally best to choose one model in the line to sell. Since you are allotted only about 12 to 20 minutes for your complete presentation, you will not have time to present several different products in the line.

Be sure your professor approves your selection. Make sure it is suitable for a sales call where you meet with the prospect at his or her home or place of business. A presentation that assumes the customer is coming to you, such as in a retail store, is not appropriate. Ask your professor when he or she expects you to have made a selection. The sooner you decide, the sooner you can begin securing the information you need to develop your presentation.

Here are some examples of products and services that students have used for their presentations.

PRODUCT EXAMPLES

Sell for . . .	Product	Sell to . . .
Food broker or food manufacturer	New food product	Grocery store chain buyer
Office supply distributor	Electronic typewriter, copier, or facsimile (FAX) machine	Office manager of a large company
Shoe manufacturer	New brand of shoe	Owner of a shoe store
Tennis racquet distributor or manufacturer	Tennis racquet	Buyer at a sporting goods store
Water ski distributor or manufacturer	Water skis	Buyer at a sporting goods store
Direct sales firm	Household cleaning product	Homeowner
Foodservice wholesaler	New food product	Food and beverage manager of a restaurant
Electronics distributor or manufacturer	Television, stereo, or videocassette recorder	Buyer at an appliance store
Golf equipment distributor or manufacturer	Golf clubs	Manager at a pro shop
Distributor of industrial cleaning products	Cleaning solvent	Purchasing agent at a large manufacturer
Communications equipment distributor	Telephone system	Office manager
Security equipment distributor	Burglar alarm or video surveillance system	Plant security manager at a large manufacturing firm
Greeting cards manufacturer	Greeting cards	Owner of a gift shop
Hardware distributor	Electric drill	Buyer for a chain of hardware stores
College textbook publisher	A new textbook on principles of selling	Professor in the marketing department
Auto parts distributor	Carburetor	Parts manager at a car dealership
Distributor or manufacturer of office partitions	Office partitions	Manager of an office building
Hot tub distributor	Hot tub	Homeowner
Sailboard distributor or manufacturer	Sailboard	Owner of a windsport shop
Archery equipment distributor	Hunting bow	Owner of a sporting goods store
Bicycle distributor or manufacturer	Racing bike	Buyer for a chain of bicycle shops
Pharmaceutical manufacturer	Prescription drug	Doctor
Communications equipment distributor	Cellular car phone	Real estate agent

PRODUCT EXAMPLES

Sell for . . .	Product	Sell to . . .
Recreational products manufacturer	Tent trailers	Recreational vehicle dealer
Life insurance company	Group life insurance or pension plan for employees	Personnel manager at a large manufacturing firm
Health maintenance organization	Group health plan	Personnel manager at your college or university
Securities and investments firm	Retirement programs	A business executive

SERVICE EXAMPLES

	Sell for . . .	Service	Sell to . . .
✓	Large hotel	Convention facilities and meeting rooms	Sales manager who is planning a sales meeting
	Radio or television station	Advertising time	Owner of a retail store
	Truck rental or leasing firm	Truck leasing	Distribution manager
	Personnel placement agency	Executive recruiting	President of a large firm
	Secretarial service	Temporary secretarial help	Personnel manager of an accounting firm
	Your college or university	College education	Guidance counselor at a local high school
	Construction contractor	Construction of an office building	President of an expanding firm
	Travel agency	Executive travel and hotel accommodations	Sales manager
	Landscape contractor	Commercial landscaping	President of a firm building a new office complex
	Real estate firm	Time-sharing condominiums	A couple in their mid-30s
	Your local newspaper or college newspaper	Advertising space	Owner of a jeans shop
	Outdoor billboard advertising firm	Advertising space	Owner of a car dealership
	Freight forwarder	Transporting goods to customers	Distribution manager at a steel fabricating plant
	Health club	Physical fitness programs conducted for employees	Personnel manager at a large publishing firm
	Florist	Plants to decorate an office	Office manager of a new bank branch
	Janitorial service	Cleaning office buildings	Office manager at a law firm
	Roofing and siding contractor	Aluminum siding	Homeowner
	Accounting and bookkeeping service	Bookkeeping	President of a wholesaling firm
	Rock and roll band	Live entertainment	Manager of a country club
	Printing and typesetting firm	Typesetting	Advertising agency
	Solar heating contractor	Solar panels	Homeowner
	Tour guide	Group tours to Europe	President of a large club
	Real estate firm	Listing a house	Homeowner

ACQUIRING BACKGROUND INFORMATION

What Information Is Needed?

To prepare a sales presentation, you must gather detailed information about the industry your firm participates in, the company you are selling for, the company and person you are selling to, the product or service you are selling, and the competitive product or service you are selling against.

A list of the information you must secure begins on page 11. Some of the sections may not apply to what you are selling. If any of the information is considered confidential by the people you meet with, note this in your report. *The more information you get, the less time it will take to develop a presentation and the higher the quality of your presentation will be.* Do not take any shortcuts or you will pay the price later in the semester. The section called "Sources of Information," beginning on page 14, explains where to get the information you need.

Availability of Information

As you can see from the list that follows, the amount of information needed to develop a good sales presentation is quite extensive. Some students encounter a great deal of difficulty securing this information. For example, their colleges or universities may be located in rural areas so that they do not have access to many businesses that are appropriate for the project. Others lack transportation so it is difficult to meet with company sources.

If you have difficulty gathering background information, the Competitive Strategy Institute has assembled a packet of information that will help you develop a good presentation. It includes brochures and other printed literature about an actual company and a product or service it markets. Information about a prospect and competitor product or service is also included. Companies, products, and services are changed periodically to provide new resources for students. Library sources are provided concerning articles written about the company, industry, and competitor. Suggestions are also provided on how to organize the information and create effective visual aids. The packet of materials does not include a typewritten report or a completed Features-Benefits Worksheet such as that on pages 133 and 134. You will be responsible for extracting appropriate information from that provided and organizing it into an effective presentation.

Background Information Order Form   To order your packet of information for your sales presentation project, complete the form below. It serves as a shipping label, so provide all the information, including your zip code, and print legibly. Include your telephone number so you can be contacted if the address is incomplete or illegible.

Send the completed form and a check or money order for $28.85 (U.S. currency) payable to Competitive Strategy Institute to the address below. This price includes the investment for the packet of information, handling charges, sales tax, and special two-day "Priority Mail" shipping charges. If you live outside the continental United States, send an additional $5.00 (U.S. currency) for extra postage.

Professor's Name _____

Class Hour _____

Amount remitted $ _____ (U.S. currency)

Competitive Strategy Institute
430 Gladstone, SE
Grand Rapids, MI U.S.A. 49506-2815

                                           Telephone No. _____
(Please Print)   Area Code

TO: _____ (Your name.)

  _____ (Residence hall and apartment/
  _____ room number, if any)
                                              (College or university)

  _____ (Street address or P.O. box)

  _____ (City, state, country)

              _____ (Zip code!)

Industry Information (the industry your company participates in)

1. What is the history of the industry from its inception to today?
2. What is the size of the total industry in terms of sales? Is the industry growing? Secure copies of articles that discuss the growth of the industry.
3. What advancements have been made in the industry in recent years?

Refer to pages 14 through 16 for sources of this information.

Company Information (the company you are selling for)

1. What is the history of your company? When was the business founded and who founded it? How has it changed throughout its history? What major accomplishments has the company experienced in recent years? Secure articles that have been published about the company and its products or services.
2. What is the size of the firm in terms of the number of employees and sales (if not confidential)? If this is a publicly held company, secure a copy of its annual report to stockholders. If this is a small company, secure some biographical information about the president and top executives. How are these individuals qualified to manage a successful business?
3. What products or services does the firm offer in its line? Be specific. Secure a catalog, brochure, or list of these products or services. Choose a product or service you will sell for your project.
4. What types of customers buy from this firm? Secure a list of local customers of this firm.
5. Does the firm have branch offices or distribution centers? If so, where are they located?
6. How many sales representatives does the firm employ in the local area? Secure literature that is used to train salespeople. Find out what is considered appropriate attire for salespeople.
7. During what months of the year does the firm enjoy its highest sales?
8. What is the firm's policy on extending credit to its customers? Are payment plans available?
9. If the sales representatives of your company have an order form or contract that customers sign, get a copy of it.
10. Secure photographs of the office building and company personnel, if available.
11. List several reasons why customers should buy from this firm. Be specific.

Refer to pages 14 through 16 for the sources of this information.

Prospect Information (the company and person you are selling to)

1. If you are selling to a business firm, choose an actual local customer your company does business with and gather the following information for that firm:
    A. The firm:
        (1) What type of organization is it (e.g., manufacturer, wholesaler, retailer, service firm)?

   (2) How large is the firm in terms of the number of employees and sales volume (if not confidential)? How long has it been in business?

   (3) What product lines or services does it sell? Be specific.

   (4) Secure any printed material about the company and its products or services, such as booklets, catalogs, and brochures.

  B. The decision maker at this firm:

   (1) Who makes the buying decisions for your product or service at this firm? What are the person's title and major responsibilities?

   (2) What are the problems and needs of this firm, and how can your product or service solve the problems or satisfy the needs? Be as detailed and specific as possible. Identify several problems and needs. What is the most important problem or need? Refer to the discussion of problems and needs in Chapter 6, beginning on page 45.

   (3) How will your product or service be used by the prospect?

  C. If you are selling a product to a wholesaler or retailer, who will resell it to the ultimate consumer, (e.g., food product or stereo):

   (1) What are the characteristics of the typical consumer, such as age, income, education, sex, family status, and occupation?

   (2) What problems or needs does the consumer have that are related to your product? Be as detailed as possible. Identify several problems and needs. What is the most important problem or need?

 2. If you are selling directly to the ultimate consumer, answer the questions in section C above. The "ultimate consumer" is someone who buys a product or service for his or her own personal consumption, such as buying a food product to eat, rather than for a restaurant.

Refer to pages 14 through 16 for sources of information.

Product/Service Information (what you are selling)

 1. General information:

  A. Have sales for this product or service been growing or declining? By how much?

  B. Does the firm offer any warranties or guarantees? Get samples of the warranty or guarantee statements.

  C. What price does your firm charge for its product or service? What discounts are offered? Secure a price list.

  D. How quickly can your company deliver its products or perform its service from the date you write the order?

  E. What are the typical reasons your company's customers give for not buying the product or service? Identify several. How does the salesperson resolve each customer objection?

  F. What proof sources do salespeople use to convince prospects to buy (e.g., marketing research studies, product or user tests, test market data, and endorsements from authorities or prominent people in the industry)? Secure some letters sent to your company from satisfied customers (i.e., testimonial letters). Ask a salesperson to tell you about two local customers who have had good results with the product or service (case histories). Find out the specific details, including who, what, when, where, and how.

  G. What visual and audio aids do your salespeople use during sales presentations, which are not mentioned elsewhere in this chapter (e.g., charts, graphs, flip charts, slides, and posters)? Get samples of them.

      H. What advertising does the firm do, including co-op advertising? Get samples of the advertisements, photoboards or videotapes of television commercials, and audiotapes of radio commercials. Note the features and benefits in the ads and commercials. Refer to the discussion of features and benefits in Chapter 6 beginning on page 46.

      I. What is the size of the average customer purchase in dollars and/or units?

      J. What services does your company offer its customers after a sale is made, including the services its sales representatives provide? What are the specific features and benefits of these services? Be as detailed as possible.

      K. What are the typical problems customers have after the sale is made? How does your company correct these problems?

2. If you are selling a service:

      A. What activities does the service include? Explain each in detail. How does your firm customize the service to meet the specific needs of its customers?

      B. What qualifications do the employees of this firm have that make them particularly well suited to provide the service? What training have they completed? How many years of experience do they have?

      C. Where is your service located? Is it more accessible to customers than that of the competition?

      D. What are the features and benefits of these activities and qualifications, and of this location? Be specific.

3. If you are selling a product:

      A. What is the history of the product? When was it invented? What major improvements have been made in recent years?

      B. What are the physical characteristics of the product, including how it is made, the materials/ingredients it contains, and how it performs? What quality control procedures are used during manufacturing? What are the features and benefits of these factors?

      C. Can your product be demonstrated? If so, how?

      D. Get a sample, scale model, cross section, or photograph of the product. Secure a specification sheet.

      E. If you are selling a product to a wholesaler or retailer, who will resell it to the ultimate consumer:

         (1) What is the suggested retail price? What is the percentage of markup and profit margin per unit?

         (2) What turnover rate can your customer expect on your product?

         (3) What sales promotional programs does your firm offer, including point-of-sale material, contests, sweepstakes, coupons, sampling, and premiums? Get specific details and examples of each.

         (4) What product and sales training programs does your company make available to its wholesalers, retailers, or dealers?

Refer to the sources of information on pages 14 through 16.

Competitor Information (what the prospect might buy or is currently buying that competes with your product or service)

1. General information:

      A. Who are your firm's main competitors? Identify one. Secure the information that follows for this competitor.

      B. When was the competitor's firm founded? Has your company been in business longer? What is the size of the competitor in relationship to your firm? Is it growing more quickly or more slowly than your firm? Why? If this is a publicly held company, secure a copy of its annual report.

C. What is the competitor's policy on extending credit to its customers? Are your firm's policies more or less liberal?

D. What price does your competitor charge for its product or service? Secure a price list. What discounts are offered? How does it compare to the price of your product or service?

E. How quickly can your competitor deliver its product or perform its service in comparison with your firm?

F. What services does the competitor offer its customers after a sale is made? How are your services superior or inferior?

G. Secure copies of catalogs, brochures, charts, graphs, and any other printed materials that are available.

H. What are your competitor's major strengths and weaknesses?

2. If you are selling a service:

A. What activities does the competitor service include? List several. Explain each in detail. How do they compare with those your firm offers?

B. What qualifications and experience do the competitor employees have? How are your employees more or less qualified to serve customers?

C. Where is the service located? Is your service more or less accessible to customers?

3. If you are selling a product:

A. What is the history of the competitor's product? When was it invented? What major improvements have been made in recent years?

B. What products does the competitor offer that your firm does/does not?

C. Secure a sample and specification sheet of the competitor's product. How is your product superior and inferior in terms of features and benefits?

D. If you are selling a product to a wholesaler or retailer, who will resell it to the ultimate consumer:

(1) What is the percentage of markup and profit margin per unit your competitor offers wholesalers or retailers? How does it compare with yours?

(2) How does the turnover rate of your product compare with that of your competitor's product?

(3) What advertising support does your competitor offer its customers? How does it compare with yours? Get examples of the advertisements and television and radio commercials.

(4) What sales promotion programs does your competitor offer its customers? How do they compare with yours?

(5) What training programs does your competitor offer its wholesalers and retailers? How do they compare with yours?

Refer to the information that follows for the sources of this information.

Sources of Information

The information needed to develop an effective presentation, listed on the previous pages, can be obtained from personal interviews, company literature, and library sources.

Personal Interview Sources

The primary source of information for your presentation will be personal interviews with representatives of the company for which you are selling. Meet with several people who work for your company, including sales representatives, sales managers, marketing personnel, and even the company president. Explain the nature of this project and ask them the questions listed on the previous pages. Consider spending a day with a representative and observe him or her during actual sales calls. Also, ask to go on a tour of the company's facilities.

Approximately one third of the information needed concerns the prospect you will be contacting and your competitor. Ask your company personnel to identify a local customer, who can be your prospect, and one competitor. They may be able to supply adequate information concerning these companies. In all probability, however, you will have to interview sales and marketing people who work for these firms. As a last resort, call or write to these companies and request the information you need.

Another primary source to consider is the librarian at your local newspaper. He or she may have information on local companies.

Since you do not want to inconvenience the people you meet with any more than necessary, you will want to gather as much information as you can in the shortest amount of time possible. It is strongly recommended that you tape the conversations you have so you do not have to waste time taking notes. Take a tape recorder with you and enough tape for at least two hours of recording. *Ask for permission to tape the interviews.*

When you meet with your sources, you are representing yourself and your college or university. It is important that you present a professional image and dress up for these meetings. Men should wear a sport coat and tie. Women should wear a dress, skirt, or suit. Treat it like an interview. Many students have gotten job offers from the companies they have used for their project. Be on time for all appointments and meet with your sources well in advance of the date this part of the project is due. Business people often have to reschedule appointments due to unforeseen commitments. You have to find your own transportation for these meetings, and you may have to meet with your sources more than once.

Company Literature Sources

A wealth of information for your report can be secured from printed literature available from your company, prospect, and competitor. Review the visual aids and proof sources requested in the "Company Information," "Product/Service Information," and "Competitor Information" sections. Answers to many of the questions can be found in this literature.

Library Sources

Most of the industry information and some of the company, prospect, product/service, and competitor information can be found in your college, university, or local library. Review the following sources. Some of them may be on electronic data bases.

Predicast F & S Index

Business Index

Business Periodicals Index

The Wall Street Index

Encyclopedia of Associations

Standard & Poor's Industry Surveys

U.S. Industrial Outlook

Value Line Investment Surveys

Thomas Registry

Trade journals related to your industry and company

Vertical file of local businesses

"Thank You" Letters

The people you will be meeting with are busy. Typically, they enjoy meeting with college students, but it does take up their time. To show your appreciation for their time, your professor may want you to send each one a "thank you" letter. The letters must be typewritten on 8½ × 11 paper and mailed in #10 business-size envelopes. Put a stamp on each one. Be sure to type the envelopes, too. Make sure there are no typographical, spelling, or grammatical errors, and do not forget to sign the letter in ink. Your professor may wish to see the letters before they are mailed. If so, put the letters in the envelopes, but do not seal them. An example of a letter and envelope is provided on the next page.

Typewritten Report

Your professor may request that you write a paper detailing the information you gathered for this project. Ask your professor about his or her requirements concerning format, content, and length.

Robinson Hall
Davenport College
415 East Fulton
Grand Rapids, MI 49503
May 14, 19____

Mr. John Gertz
Senior Sales Representative
Wyman Distributing Company
3510 Division Avenue
Grand Rapids, MI 49506

Dear Mr. Gertz:

Please accept my sincere appreciation for all the assistance you gave me with my project for my "Principles of Selling" class. I realize you are a very busy man and you had to spend a lot of time providing me with the information I needed.

The meetings we had were both interesting and very informative. I especially want to thank you for allowing me to accompany you on several sales calls. It was exciting for me to see how the concepts I'm learning in class are applied in the real world. The product sample and visual aids you loaned me were very helpful, too.

As a result of my class project and my meetings with you, I am seriously considering a career in sales. It looks like it would be fun and provide me with substantial financial rewards if I apply what I have learned in this class.

Thank you again for your time and the knowledge you shared with me.

Sincerely,

Debbie Johnson

Debbie Johnson, Student
Davenport College

Debbie Johnson
Robinson Hall
Davenport College
415 East Fulton
Grand Rapids, MI 49503

Mr. John Gertz
Senior Sales Representative
Wyman Distributing Company
3510 Division Avenue
Grand Rapids, MI 49506

(Use a business-size envelope that measures 4-¼″ × 9-½″)

PROSPECTING AND THE PREAPPROACH

Prospecting

Before a salesperson can begin making sales calls, he or she must identify potential customers. This process is called *prospecting*. In some industries, potential customers are well defined and easy to identify. The manufacturer of packaged food products would call on grocery and convenience stores. A firm selling a typesetting service would call on printers and advertising agencies. However, determining who to call on if you are selling life insurance, meeting rooms and convention facilities, or aluminum siding for homes would be more challenging. Some salespeople spend as much as 80 percent of their time prospecting.

If you were hired to represent Brooks Shoe, Inc., in your state, who would you call on to sell Fusion, a new running shoe? Shoe stores and sporting goods stores might come to mind, but which specific stores? What are the store names, addresses, and telephone numbers? What are the names of the buyers? What sources would you explore to identify these stores? Your first source would be the list of current customers Brooks would give you. A trade publication called *Sporting Goods Buyers' Directory* would also be a good source. It lists all the sporting goods stores in the United States, by state and city. Store names, addresses, telephone numbers, and buyers' names are provided. You might identify some prospects as you are driving around your territory. National and regional sporting goods trade shows can be an excellent source for prospects. Finally, some of your current customers may open new stores. These are possible prospects, provided they are located in your territory.

Prospecting must be a continuous process, because salespeople lose customers even if they represent excellent companies and sell superior products or services. Customers may move out of their territory, buyers may change jobs, competitors may take customers, and customers may become bad credit risks or even go out of business. Most firms lose 10 to 25 percent of their customers each year. If a firm had 1,000 customers today, lost only 10 percent each year, and did not replace any, it would have only 590 customers in five years. Note the figure on the following page.

Qualifying

Qualifying is the process of gathering information about a potential customer to determine if it is worthwhile to make fact-to-face sales presentation. Specifically, you are trying to determine whether the customer has a need for your product or service, has the financial resources to pay for it, and will purchase quantities large enough to make the customer profitable, as well as whether the person you are calling on has the authority to make a purchase decision. It would be a waste of time to call on a firm that did not meet these four criteria. The information gathered while qualifying a potential customer has the added benefit of helping

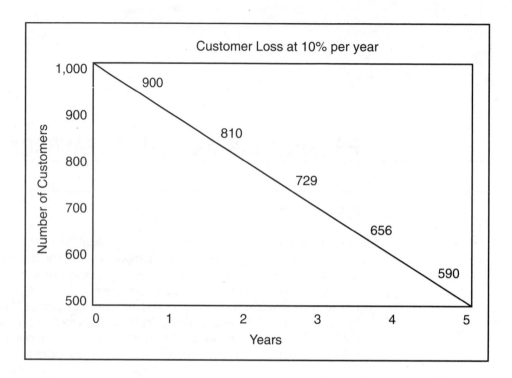

you plan what to say during the sales call. A potential customer, who has been qualified, is called a *prospect*.

The Preapproach

The preapproach involves securing an appointment to make the presentation, developing a profile of the prospect, determining your sales call objective, and planning the presentation. The process of planning the presentation is discussed in Chapters 5 through 8. The other features of the preapproach are discussed next.

Securing the Appointment

Before you can make a sales presentation, you must secure an appointment with the prospect. In some cases, this can be more challenging than convincing a prospect to buy. There are three methods salespeople use to secure appointments. They are cold calling in person, telephone prospecting, and sending a letter of introduction followed by a telephone call.

Cold calling in person involves walking into a prospect's place of business without an appointment. An advantage to cold calling is that you can reduce travel time by calling on all the businesses in an area. Cold calling is also an effective method of getting appointments with prospects who will not grant them over the telephone. Qualifying and profiling information can be gathered on cold calls as well.

There are, however, many disadvantages to this method of getting appointments. Some prospects will not see salespeople without an appointment. In such cases, the most you can hope for on a cold call is to secure an appointment for a later date. Cold calling is very time-consuming. Prospects may not be available when you arrive. Finally, cold calling may not be appropriate if you are selling certain things, such as high-priced, technical products or services, including computer software and health insurance. Prospects in these fields may consider cold calling to be unprofessional.

An increasing number of salespeople are using the telephone to secure appointments. Telephone prospecting is inexpensive and less time-consuming than cold calling, because you can cover a large number of geographically dispersed prospects in a relatively short time. Disadvantages to this method are that it is easier for a prospect to say "no" on the telephone than in person, and you do not have the benefit of observing the prospect's non-verbal communications. Furthermore, some salespeople have difficulty dealing with rejection on the telephone. Ten telephone calls might result in talking to five decision makers, with two consenting to an appointment.

A procedure that will increase the productivity of telephone prospecting is sending a letter of introduction prior to the call. The letter will prepare the prospect for the call and will help convey a professional image for you and your company. Referring to the letter during the telephone call will also help you establish a rapport.

The purpose of the letter should be to get the prospect's attention and to arouse interest in and anticipation of your telephone call. It must be addressed to a specific individual and should focus on one or two important benefits. Do not disclose too much information. The letter is intended to increase your chance of securing an appointment, not to close the sale. A sample letter of introduction, to try to get an appointment for Brooks with a sporting goods buyer appears on page 22.

A dialogue of a telephone call between Jeff Dykehouse, who is selling Fusion, and Penny Taylor, a sporting goods buyer, is provided next to help illustrate what a call might sound like. Assume she was sent the letter on page 22 prior to the call. A detailed discussion of telephone prospecting is provided in Chapter 10. It was not presented here, because an understanding of the concepts discussed in Chapters 5 through 8 is necessary for you to understand what to say during a telephone call.

JEFF:	Ms. Taylor?
PROSPECT:	Yes.
JEFF:	My name is Jeff Dykehouse from Brooks Shoe Company. How are you today?
PROSPECT:	Pretty good.
JEFF:	Last Monday, I sent you a letter concerning our exciting new running shoe called Fusion. Do you remember seeing it?
PROSPECT:	Yes.
JEFF:	You'll recall that in the letter I mentioned Fusion has a new patented feature that will improve the running performance of your customers while reducing injuries. I'm calling to see when we can get together to explain how Fusion will increase your athletic shoes sales and profits.
	Ms. Taylor, are mornings or afternoons best for you?
PROSPECT:	We don't need any more running shoes right now.
JEFF:	You are definitely in a position to know if you need any new products, Ms. Taylor. However, the real question is whether you are open to a product that is a true breakthrough in running shoe technology. One that your customers will love and that will provide more profits for your store.

▶BROOKS.

January 22, 19_____

Ms. Penny Taylor
Taylor Sports, Inc.
2122 Main Street
Grand Rapids, MI 49507

Dear Ms. Taylor:

Are your customers looking for an athletic shoe that will improve running performance and reduce foot, ankle, and leg injuries? Are you looking for a shoe that will generate more profits for your store?

Brooks is about to launch a revolutionary new running shoe called Fusion. Perhaps you have read about Fusion in the trade press or heard that it recently won the "Best Running Shoe" award at the EXSL show in Europe. Fusion has a special patented feature, which is a breakthrough in running shoe technology.

The whole story is especially exciting. In the next week, I'll call you to arrange a time to show you Fusion. When we meet, I will also explain the details of our comprehensive marketing program planned to support Fusion and show how it will increase your athletic shoe sales and profits.

Sincerely,

Jeffery Dykehouse

Jeffery Dykehouse

Would next Tuesday or Wednesday morning be more convenient for you?

PROSPECT: I guess I could meet with you on Wednesday at 10:30.

JEFF: Great! Your office is located at 2122 Main Street, right?

PROSPECT: Yes. That's right.

JEFF: I look forward to meeting you next Wednesday at 10:30, Ms. Taylor.

Developing a Profile of the Prospect

The type of presentation you are developing is called *need satisfaction selling*. The entire presentation revolves around a *specific* prospect's needs. It is customized and reflects the prospect's personality, current situation, purchases of competitor products and services, and problems. To customize a presentation, you must know something about the firm and the individual you are calling on before planning the presentation and making the sales call. A prospect profile must be completed. The profile will result in asking the right questions and providing the appropriate features and benefits during the presentation, which will increase the probability that you will close the sale.

Gathering profiling information before the sales call is challenging because often it is not readily available. Secondary sources on pages 15 and 16 can be explored. Primary sources include current customers, competitor sales representatives, receptionists and secretaries at the prospect's place of business, and the actual prospect. Some profile information cannot be secured until the sales call. The more information that can be gathered before the initial call, the greater the chances of the call being successful.

Companies often provide their salespeople with a prospect profile form. The one that follows is for Brooks. Study it thoroughly so that you can gain a better understanding of the continuing case.

BROOKS PROSPECT PROFILE

Company Name: __Taylor Sports, Inc.__

Address: __2122 Main Street__

__Grand Rapids, MI__   Zip Code: __49507__

Telephone Number: __(616) 555-2122__

Location/Direction/Travel Time: __Route 67 to Trobridge exit. North on Trobridge__
__two miles to Lakewood Shopping Plaza. Travel Time—1 hour 15 minutes__

Company Sales Volume: __N.A.__   Number of Stores: __1__

Years in Business: __6 months__   Credit Rating: __N.A.__

Decision Maker's Name/Title: __Ms. Penny Taylor, owner with Bill Winston__

Major Responsibilities: __Manages the store. Buys athletic shoes. (Bill buys other__
__sports products.)__

Personal Qualities of Decision Maker: __Sounded like a dominant personality__
__on the phone.__

Best Time to See: __Tuesday and Wednesday mornings__

Names/Titles of Others Who Influence Buying Decisions: __None__

Secretary's Name: __None__

Current Shoe Lines: __Nike, Asics, Etonic, and Reebok. The store has never ordered__
__from Brooks.__

Target Market: __This is a specialty sporting goods store which appeals to the__
__serious recreational athlete.__

Trading Area: __Ten-mile radius of the store__

Problems/Needs: __Increase sales and profits, generate more store traffic, stock__
__running shoes that appeal to the serious runner__

Determining the Sales Call Objective

Before you meet with your prospect, you must decide what you hope to achieve during the sales call. This is called the *sales call objective*. Think of it as a target. To hit a target you must be able to see it. Even a world champion archer cannot hit a target unless he can see it. So the sales call objective should be written down before each call. It should be specific, measurable, and a time frame must be provided showing when the plan of action will be implemented. Following is the sales call objective for Fusion. Other examples are provided to help you develop your own sales call objective.

> Fusion Sales Call Objective: Convince the athletic shoe buyer to buy 18 pairs of the Fusion running shoe, price them at $124.95 per pair, and accept delivery by the first of next month.

You Are Selling . . .	Sales Call Objective
An employee fitness program to the human resources director of a large firm	Convince the prospect to buy 10 health club memberships for the firm's top executives with fitness evaluations to be conducted next week.
A sales training workshop to a district sales manager	Convince the prospect to schedule a two-day workshop for 27 new and experienced sales representatives during the week of November 15.
An industrial cleaning solvent to a purchasing agent at a large manufacturer	Convince the prospect to buy a sample quantity of Quick-Cleen for testing, accept delivery by next week, and have the test completed by the end of the month.
A new prescription drug to a doctor	Convince the doctor to accept 50 free samples of Inoxcine today, begin dispensing the samples to his patients, and begin prescribing the medication through his patients' pharmacies immediately.
A new food product to the food and beverage manager of a restaurant	Convince the prospect to buy 5 cases of Bostonian Frozen Shrimp, accept delivery by Friday, and add the item to the menu immediately.
Meeting room facilities to a sales manager who is planning a sales meeting	Convince the prospect to accompany me to my hotel this week to see the meeting rooms and sample various items on our luncheon menu.
College education to a high school counselor	Convince the prospect to bring 20 students to my campus by the end of the month for a tour, orientation, and lunch.
A new food product to a grocery store chain buyer	Convince the prospect to buy 20 cases/store of Pep, display the product on the shelf in the diet section of the store, price it $1.79, and accept delivery by next week.
Construction services to the president of a firm that is planning to build an addition to its plant	Convince the prospect to allow my firm to submit a bid for this construction project on the first of the month.

(continued)

You Are Selling . . .	Sales Call Objective
Radio time to the owner of a clothing store	Convince the prospect to sign a contract for 50 thirty-second radio spots to air next month.
A pre-packaged tour of Europe to the assistant minister of a large church.	Convince the prospect to allow me to make a slide presentation next week to people in the congregation who are interested in such a vacation.
A fleet of automobiles to a large food manufacturer	Convince the prospect to accompany me to my dealership this week to test ride the Oldsmobile Cutlass.
Group life insurance to the personnel manager of a large manufacturer	Convince the prospect to allow me to do a needs analysis of the firm this week so I can present a group life plan by the first of the month.

In the space provided below, write the sales call objective for your product or service.

MY SALES CALL OBJECTIVE IS:

Planning the Sales Presentation

A sales call must be well planned if it is going to be successful. The information to communicate during the call must be gathered and organized in a logical sequence to change the prospect from being unaware of your company and product or service to being willing to buy. Appropriate questions must be identified to ascertain the prospect's current situation and needs. Visual aids must be developed to enhance your ability to communicate your message. Questions and resistance the prospect might offer must be anticipated. Everything you plan to say and do must be determined ahead of time. Final preparation involves practicing the presentation before the call.

The next few chapters will help you plan your sales presentation. The presentation is divided into four sections: Approach, Securing Desire, Handling Objections, and Closing the Sale. In Chapter 5, on the Approach, you will learn how to introduce yourself to the prospect, establish a rapport, gain his or her interest and attention, and begin to gather information related to his or her current situation. Chapter 6, "Securing Desire," is where the body of the presentation is discussed. Prospect problems and needs are identified and supported with features and benefits. Chapter 7 is called "Handling Objections". You will identify the resistance your prospect may offer and learn how to overcome it. Chapter 8, on Closing the Sale, will provide insight on how to ask for a commitment. Plenty of examples are included to help you step-by-step through the process of building your presentation. Opportunities will also be presented for you to practice the presentation using sophisticated role playing techniques.

chapter 5

OPENING YOUR SALES PRESENTATION

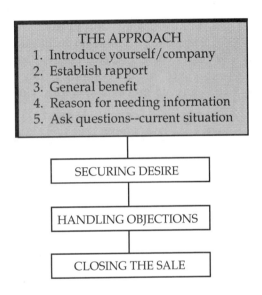

Objectives of the Approach

The opening of your presentation is your first opportunity to meet the prospect face to face. It is the most important part of your presentation because if you do not do it effectively, the prospect will not allow you to make a complete presentation. The first 30 seconds are the most critical because you are setting the stage for what is to follow.

When you walk into the prospect's office, he or she is typically in the middle of doing something else. You must direct attention and interest away from this activity to what you have to say. You must also establish an immediate rapport with the prospect and answer the question on every buyer's mind: "What's in this meeting for me?" Finally, you must gather information about the prospect, so you can tailor the body of the presentation around the current situation.

You should make certain assumptions concerning the prospect:

1. You are calling on one person, not a group, and you have never met the prospect. The prospect has never done business with your firm.

2. You called the prospect on the telephone a week ago and set up this appointment.

3. You were able to qualify him or her as a potential prospect. He or she is the primary decision maker and has a potential need for your product or service.

Questioning Skills

One of the most important goals of a sales presentation is to establish two-way communications with the prospect. Questions are used to solicit prospect responses.

There are many benefits to asking questions and establishing a dialogue. Since this is the first meeting with the prospect, questions that provide an opportunity for the prospect to talk will help reduce some of the tension. These questions help you to get acquainted. Questions help keep the prospect's attention and get him or her involved in the presentation. They show that you are interested and also allow you to gather important information necessary in light of his or her situation, problems, and needs.

There are two basic forms of questions. Open questions begin with "who," "what," "when," "where," "why," "which," and "how." They cannot be answered with a "yes" or "no" response. They require the prospect to explain or elaborate, and thus are excellent ways to begin a dialogue or solicit information.

Who are you buying from now?

What problems have you encountered with your current supplier?

When will you have the time to talk to the buying committee?

Where are your distribution centers located?

Why do you use this service?

Which lines are selling the best in your stores?

How often do you need quick delivery?

Closed questions, on the other hand, elicit "yes" or "no" responses. They are used to direct the flow of communication in a specific direction, check for understanding, and get a commitment. Closed questions begin with "is," "do," "does," "are," "can," "may," "will," "has," "have," "would," "should," and "were."

Is someone else involved in the decision making?

Does this resolve your concern about price?

Are you satisfied with the quality of service you are getting?

Can your current supplier guarantee delivery in two weeks' time?

Will delivery next week be soon enough?

Has another firm approached you about this type of service?

Would you say this is what you want?

Were you prepared to make a decision today?

You will be using open and closed questions throughout the presentation to establish a rapport with the prospect, gather facts, discover needs, confirm agreement, elicit reactions or buying signals, and close the sale. While these will be discussed in detail later, the following examples will help you better understand the questioning process in a sales presentation.

Rapport-building questions are open or closed questions that help you to get acquainted with the prospect and better understand his or her personality.

Fact-finding questions solicit information about the prospect's current situation. They can be open questions such as "From whom are you currently buying?" or closed questions such as "Do you stock XYZ brand?"

Need-discovery questions are used to uncover buying motives. "What type of profit margin do you expect?" is an example of an open question. "Would you like to save 10% in your distribution costs?" is a closed question.

Confirming questions check for understanding or solicit agreement. They are generally closed questions such as "Can I assume you would like to solve that problem?"

Elaboration questions ask the prospect to explain something in greater detail, such as "Would you tell me more?" or "Could you elaborate on that point?"

Trial close questions are used to determine the prospect's readiness to buy. They measure the prospect's buying temperature. "What's your reaction to what I've said so far?" is an example.

Closing questions ask for a commitment that will allow the salesperson to achieve the sales call objective. "May we begin to provide our service to you starting next week?"

Listening

Listening is a very important aspect of effective communication, but many people are poor listeners. This is partially due to the fact that people speak at a rate of 120 to 150 words per minute, while our minds can absorb 600 words per minute. It is also a result of not understanding the importance of effective listening and not knowing how to listen.

Are you a poor listener? Do you avoid eye contact when someone is speaking to you? Do you engage in physical activity or let your mind wander? Do you make judgments about what is being said before the speaker is finished? Do you nonverbally convey the impression that you are impatient or interrupt the speaker before he or she is finished? Do you give the impression that you do not care about what is being said? If you are like most people and have developed some bad listening habits, start practicing some of these techniques in your personal and professional life:

1. Maintain eye contact.
2. If you are engaged in an activity when someone begins talking to you, stop what you are doing. Listen!
3. Focus your attention on what is being said. Be alert. Also, listen for what is *not* being said. Summarize the main ideas in your mind.
4. Withhold judgment. Try to keep an open mind. Do not judge prematurely.
5. Relax and be patient with the speaker.
6. Practice active listening techniques.

Active listening involves conveying verbally and nonverbally that you are interested in and understand what the speaker is saying. Showing interest demonstrates that you think the speaker is an important person and worth listening to. Checking for understanding will ensure that your responses or future actions are appropriate. Here are some active listening techniques that you should use:

1. Periodically nod your head in agreement.
2. Tilt your head to the side as if to point your ear toward the speaker.
3. React to what is being said and encourage the speaker by saying things like "Really?"; "Great"; "That's interesting"; "I see"; "Uh-huh"; "Is that so?" and "Tell me more."

4. Echo the last words the person said, such as "Your sales are up 20%?"

5. Paraphrase your understanding of what the speaker said. You might make a comment like, "It sounds like you're looking for. . . ."

6. Ask questions related to what was said.

The discussion that follows explains what to say during the Approach portion of your sales presentation. Be sure to use the questioning and listening techniques discussed previously in this and the other three parts of the presentation.

Steps in the Approach

Step 1. Introduce Yourself and Your Company and Present Your Business Card

The first impression you make when you greet the prospect is very important. Dress appropriately for the product or service you are selling. Put your visual aids in a folder, loose-leaf binder, or attaché case. Do not put your attaché case on the prospect's desk. Keep it on your lap or on the floor. If you have a sample of your product, do not reveal it until the Securing Desire section of the presentation. When you enter the prospect's office, maintain good posture, project self-confidence, and maintain eye contact. Smile and be enthusiastic. The following is how to conduct a good introduction.

1. *Greet the prospect by stating his name.* A general rule is to use "Mr.," "Mrs.," or "Ms." and the person's last name, unless there is a clear sign that it is appropriate to use the first name. If the prospect seems to have a friendly personality and is approximately your age and of your social standing, it might be appropriate to use a first name. Be sure to pronounce the name correctly.

2. *State your name and company name* slowly and clearly so it can be understood.

3. *Shake the prospect's hand, if appropriate.* A proper handshake is one of the ways you can begin to break down some of the barriers of communication. It helps create a friendly atmosphere. You should grip the prospect's entire hand and not just the fingers. The handshake should be firm, but not a "bone crusher." Men can initiate a handshake with women and women can initiate it with men. If you sense the prospect is not comfortable with a handshake, wait for him or her to initiate it.

4. *Offer your business card.* Some sales trainers recommend that the business card be given to the prospect at the end of the presentation, because it can be a distraction. The benefit to offering it early is that the prospect will feel more comfortable with this means of remembering your name and your company name. A business card for use during your role plays is provided on the inside front cover of this text.

5. *Be seated.* If the prospect's demeanor and his or her office setting seem to be informal, sit in a chair as close to him or her as possible without asking for permission. If the atmosphere seems formal ask "May I have a seat?"

Step 2. Establish a Rapport

Now you want to reduce the relationship tension and create an atmosphere conducive to buying. You want to "break the ice" so you and the prospect can relax. Bring up something informal that does not necessarily relate to your sales call objective. Never ask, "How's business?" Many salespeople use this icebreaker, and prospects get tired of answering the same question all the time. Openings related to sports are overused, too. Try to be original and spontaneous, focusing on the prospect's interests, not yours. Remember, get him or her talking for 30 seconds to one minute. Start with open questions. Here are some examples of icebreakers:

1. *A sincere compliment.* "On my way in to see you this morning, Mr. Ryan, I noticed the attractive window display by the checkout. Who designs your displays for you? How do you choose which clothing to display? Do you think the display has a big impact on traffic and sales?

2. *An acquaintance.* "Mrs. Michael, the other day I was over at Apex Products, and Sue Monroe mentioned she knew you. How do you know her? I know Sue plays a lot of golf. Do you ever play golf with her?

3. *Something you observe.* This could be something you saw in the parking lot, lobby, or buyer's office. "I can see from the pictures on the wall, Mr. Taylor, you're a sailor. What kind of a boat is that? Is it yours? How often do you get a chance to go sailing? Have you ever raced? How did you do?"

4. *Current events.* "I noticed in the paper, Mrs. Peterson, your company had its 50th anniversary last month. How did you celebrate? How many people attended? Who organized it? Was it successful?"

Let the conversation lead naturally to a conclusion and provide a transition to Step 3. For example, if you were talking about golf, you could say "I've been wanting to take up golf for some time. Perhaps I'll have a chance to try it this summer."

The prospect may have a dominant personality or be pressed for time. He or she may want to dispense with the small talk and get down to business. If so, skip this step and proceed to Step 3, but look for an opening later in the presentation when you can establish a rapport.

Step 3. State Your Purpose and General Benefit

The purpose of this step is to give the prospect an idea of where you are going and to provide a reason why he or she should listen. You should get his or her attention and arouse curiosity. The general benefit is a brief question or statement, which reflects what the prospect will ultimately gain by listening to your presentation. It answers the prospect's question, "What's in it for me?" It has to focus on a general problem or need, because you do not know what the specific needs are yet. The following is a list of general problems or needs for businesses and consumers.

General Problems and Needs For Businesses

Increase sales and profits

Reduce costs

Increase employee productivity

Improve product quality

Get better service

Save time

Improve efficiency

Reduce inventories

Improve store traffic and turnover

Improve awareness of the firm

Save the environment

Improve safety or security

Reduce employee turnover

Improve the quality of work life

General Problems and Needs For Consumers

Save money

Increase income

Save time

Gain prestige

Improve protection and security

Experience pride of ownership

Seek companionship

Advance in one's career

Gain approval

The general benefit should be concise, not more than one or two sentences—just enough to whet the prospect's appetite. It should be as specific as possible and conveyed in a dramatic way. If you are selling to a retailer or distributor, and your product will be resold, the general benefit should probably include a reference to profits and a benefit for the end user, such as the general benefit example for the sporting goods buyer that follows. The general benefit statement may be the only part of your presentation that should be memorized. The words must be chosen carefully and must be well organized. Here are some examples of general benefit statements:

Prospect	General Benefit Statement
Sporting goods buyer	"Ms. Taylor, I'm here today to show you our atheletic shoe, called Fusion, which will improve the running performance of your customers, significantly reduce foot and knee injuries, and provide you with over $1,500 in profits this season."
Purchasing agent at a large manufacturing firm	"What I would like to do today, Dave, is show you how our new cleaning solvent will cut the amount of time it takes your people to clean the floors in your office area by 30%. This time savings will save you about $1,200 in the next year."
Owner of a retail store	"Mrs. Jones, how would you like to get 15% more advertising exposure with your target market and more traffic to your store without increasing your ad budget?"
A couple in their mid-30's interested in time-sharing condominiums	"Mr. and Mrs. Wiley, the reason I stopped by tonight was to show you how you can buy your own condominium in beautiful Hawaii for an investment of only $25,000."

(continued)

Prospect	General Benefit Statement
Personnel manager of a large publishing firm considering a physical fitness program for the firm's executives	"Al, I'd like to share with you some details about how you can improve the productivity and effectiveness of your top executives as much as 10%."
A business executive interested in a retirement program	"Mr. Douglas, how would you like to never have to worry about your financial needs during retirement?"
District sales manager, who is responsible for 30 sales representatives	"Nancy Gerts over at JGC and Associates recommended that I tell you about the workshop we offer. Her sales representatives experienced a 15 percent increase in sales after completing the course."
President of a medium-sized firm	"The banquet facilities at our hotel are perfect for your upcoming employee Christmas party, Mr. Martin. I'd like to show you how we can make it a very memorable occasion, and how we can save you money, too."

Step 4. Explain Your Reason for Needing Information

In Step 5 you will ask the prospect several questions to learn about his or her current situation. The prospect may be reluctant to share this information unless you explain why you need it. Here are some examples of how to persuade the prospect to answer your questions.

"To find out how we can increase your profits, can I ask you a few questions?"

"Is it okay to ask you some questions about your business? That way I can recommend a program that will meet your specific needs."

Step 5. Ask Fact-Finding Questions to Determine the Prospect's Current Situation

The purpose of this step is to learn enough about the prospect so that the information you provide in the Securing Desire section will be relevant to this prospect's situation. You are trying to find out about:

1. The prospect
2. The prospect's company
3. Which of your competitors the prospect is currently doing business with, if any
4. What competitor product or service the prospect is using now.

Only ask questions that are relevant to the information you need for your presentation. At this point, do not try to identify problems or needs the prospect may have—save that for the Securing Desire section of the presentation. Start with a series of open questions and end with closed questions. Do not ask too many closed questions in a row because the prospect will feel like you are interrogating him or her. You should have about three to five questions. Here are examples of the fact-finding questions you would ask if you were selling Fusion shoes to a buyer at a sporting goods store, health club memberships to a firm's manager of human resources, and a sales training workshop to a sales manager.

Running Shoes

    "How many brands of running shoes do you currently stock?"

    "Which brands are your most popular?"

       "Least popular?"

    "Who is your target market?"

    "Are you considering any other new brands of running shoes at this time?"

Health Club Memberships for Executives

    "How many employees work for this company?"

    "How many employees are considered middle or upper management?"

    "Do you currently have a fitness program for executives?"

    "Have you talked to any other health clubs that offer executive fitness programs?"

    "Does your company pay the health insurance premiums for your executives?"

Sales Training Workshop

    "How many salespeople do you manage?"

    "What sales training have you done in the past?"

    "Who provided the training?"

    "Are you considering any other training programs?"

Example of the Approach

The following is an example of the Approach section of the presentation for Fusion. The "Setting the Scene" page explains the nature of the sales call. The salesperson-prospect dialog begins on page 36.

SETTING THE SCENE—FUSION RUNNING SHOES

Salesperson's Name: __Jeff Dykehouse__

Salesperson's Company Name: __Brooks Shoe, Inc.__

Product or Service Being Sold: __Fusion running shoes__

Prospect's Name: __Ms. Penny Taylor__   Title: __Owner/Manager__

Prospect's Company Name: __Taylor Sports, Inc.__

Type of Business: __Specialty retail sporting goods store__

Prospect's Major Responsibilities: __Penny manages the store and buys the athletic shoes.__

Month of the Year: __February__

Sales Call Objective: __Convince Penny to buy 18 pairs of Fusion shoes, price them at $124.95 per pair, and accept delivery by the first of next month.__

PLANNING GUIDE—FUSION APPROACH

Salesperson-Prospect Dialogue

Step 1. Introduction

SALESPERSON: *Ms. Taylor?*

PROSPECT: *Yes.*

SALESPERSON: *I'm Jeff Dykehouse with Brooks Shoe, Inc. How are you today? (Smile and be enthusiastic. Shake her hand. Present your business card. Be seated.)*

Step 2. Establish a rapport

SALESPERSON: *I can see from the pictures on the wall that you are a runner. In what races do you compete?*

PROSPECT: *Last summer I ran in the Reeds Lake Run and the Old Kent Bank Riverbank Run. I'd like to compete more often, but I just don't have the time.*

SALESPERSON: *I've run in the Reeds Lake Run, too. What distance do you usually run, Penny?*

PROSPECT: *The 5K. Anything longer than that is too hard on my body. I usually place in the top 10 or 15 in my age category.*

SALESPERSON: *That's great! By any chance are you going to the sporting goods show in Atlanta later this month?*

PROSPECT: *Not this year. My partner is going. I just can't be away from the store for four days.*

SALESPERSON: *I plan to be there. Maybe your partner can stop by our booth. What's his name?*

PROSPECT: *Bill Winston.*

SALESPERSON: *I'll have to talk to Bill and invite him to stop by.*

PLANNING GUIDE—FUSION APPROACH *(continued)*

Salesperson-Prospect Dialogue

Step 3. Purpose and general benefit statement

SALESPERSON: *Well, the reason I'm here today, Penny, is to show you our new running shoe, called Fusion. It's a technological breakthrough that will improve running performance and reduce injuries for your customers, and it will provide your store with over $1,500 in profits this spring.*

Step 4. Reason for needing information

SALESPERSON: *To find out how we can increase your profits, can I ask you a few questions?*

PROSPECT: *Okay.*

Step 5. Fact-finding questions to determine the prospect's current situation

SALESPERSON: *Penny, I noticed when I came in that you stock Nike, Asics, Etonic, and Reebok running shoes. How are they selling?*

PROSPECT: *During the running season they sell very well. Asics seem to be our top seller in the high-performance category.*

SALESPERSON: *Which brand would you say has the slowest turnover?*

PROSPECT: *I would have to say the Reebok ERS shoe. It never really caught on.*

SALESPERSON: *And who is your target market?*

PROSPECT: *Since we are a specialty sporting goods store, I would have to say we cater to the serious recreational athlete. People who shop in K Mart and Sears are not the ones we're after.*

SALESPERSON: *Are you considering any new high-performance running shoes at this time?*

PROSPECT: *The Nike rep was in last week and showed me the new 180 Air. It looks pretty good.*

Preparing to Role Play

Setting the Scene and Planning Guide Forms—The Approach

Now that you have learned what an effective Approach consists of, it is time to develop one for the product or service you have selected. First complete the Setting the Scene Form, using the example for Fusion on page 35 as a guide. This form will be used to orient people observing your role plays. Then complete your Planning Guide. Refer to the example for Fusion on pages 36 and 37. Provide a complete dialogue of what you and the prospect say. Be sure to complete all the forms neatly in number 2 pencil. Later on, you may want to make changes. A number 2 pencil is recommended, because hard pencils do not produce good photocopies. Look over the section on assumptions on page 27 and the rating form on page 44 to make sure you understand how the Approach should be structured and evaluated.

SETTING THE SCENE

Each time you role play, set the scene for the prospect and those observing you. Share the information that follows with them. Refer to page 35 for an example of a completed form for Fusion.

Print neatly in number 2 pencil so the information can be changed and photocopied.

Salesperson's Name: ___Jeff Dykehouse___   Hour: _____

Salesperson's Company Name: ___Brooks Shoe, Inc_____

Product or Service Being Sold: _____

_____

Prospect's Name: ___(Use role play partner's actual name)___   Title: _____

Prospect's Company Name: _____

Type of Business: _____

Prospect's Major Responsibilities: _____

_____

_____

_____

_____

Month of the Year: _____

Sales Call Objective (Refer to page 25): _____

_____

_____

_____

_____

PLANNING GUIDE—THE APPROACH

Salesperson-Prospect Dialogue

Refer to the example of the completed Planning Guide for Fusion on pages 36 and 37.

Step 1. Introduction *(Fill this form out neatly in number 2 pencil. Write small. See page 30.)*

Step 2. Establish a rapport *(See pages 30 and 31.)*

(continued)

PLANNING GUIDE—THE APPROACH *(continued)*

Salesperson-Prospect Dialogue

Step 3. Purpose and general benefit statement *(See pages 31 through 33.)* I am here to...

Step 4. Reason for needing information *(See page 33.)*

Step 5. Questions to determine current situation *(These should be fact-finding questions not ones related to the prospect's needs or problems. See pages 33 and 34.)*

How the Role Play Will Be Conducted

Your sales manager may have you role play this portion of the sales presentation. If not, you should role play it on your own to ensure you will be properly prepared for the role play of the complete presentation. If possible, role play with other people who can assume the roles of the prospect and your coach. The salesperson must provide a photocopy of his or her Planning Guide to the prospect. If a copy machine is not available, neatly print or type the salesperson-prospect dialogue for Steps 2 and 5 including the titles of the steps.

When you are role playing as the salesperson, use appropriate visual or audio aids. Your sales manager will decide whether you can refer to your Planning Guide during the role play.

When you are a prospect, refer to the salesperson's Planning Guide so you know how to respond to questions. Feel free to ad lib and make up your responses to questions for which you do not have information. The only time you will object to the salesperson is when you role play Handling Objections and during the complete presentation.

The coach will observe the role play, fill out a rating form, and critique the salesperson at the end. Fill out each section of the form as soon as the salesperson completes it rather than waiting until the end. After the role play, give the salesperson feedback on what skills need improvement. Here is how to get started:

1. Salesperson gives the prospect the photocopy of the Planning Guides so he or she can become familiar with the responses that should be provided.

2. Salesperson sets the scene for the prospect and coach by reading the information in the Setting the Scene Form on page 39.

3. Salesperson gives the coach the rating form. Space is provided to record the scores of three role plays.

4. Salesperson and prospect role play while the coach fills out the rating form.

5. Coach critiques the role play and returns the rating form to the salesperson.

To prepare for your role as salesperson, you *must rehearse the role play several times*. Say the words aloud by yourself or, better yet, to someone else. You must get used to hearing yourself play the role. Study the Planning Guide, rehearse the role play, then study the guide again so you can see what needs improvement. Use the "Steps in a Sales Presentation" guide on the inside front cover of this text to make sure you are performing the steps in the proper order. Tape yourself several times to hear what you sound like. Use the rating form to evaluate yourself.

Materials Needed to Role Play the Approach

You will need your completed Setting the Scene Form on page 39, Planning Guide, a photocopy of the two-page Planning Guide for the prospect, Approach Rating Form, business card, and *RPPS* manual. If you do not have access to a photocopy machine to reproduce your Planning Guide for the prospect, neatly print or type the salesperson-prospect dialogue for Steps 2 and 5 including the titles of the steps.

Approach Rating Form (25 Points)

Salesperson's Company: _____   Hour: _____

Product/Service: _____   Salesperson's Name: _____

Prospect's Company: _____

	Possible Score	Actual Score		
		Record Scores of Three Role Plays		
—Ability to introduce yourself and company	2	_____	_____	_____
—Ability to offer a firm handshake, present your business card, and be seated	2	_____	_____	_____
—Ability to establish a rapport by asking questions and getting the prospect to respond; ability to keep the prospect talking long enough to feel relaxed	5	_____	_____	_____
—Ability to state your purpose and general benefit	5	_____	_____	_____
—Ability to explain your reason for needing information	2	_____	_____	_____
—Ability to ask appropriate fact-finding questions to determine the prospect's current situation	5	_____	_____	_____
—Ability to be enthusiastic, smile, and to use the prospect's name	4	_____	_____	_____
Total	25 pts.	_____	_____	_____

Coach's notes and comments:

SECURING DESIRE

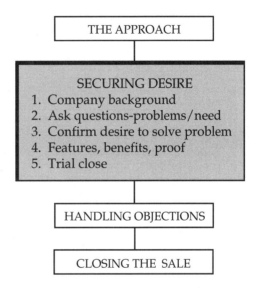

THE APPROACH

SECURING DESIRE
1. Company background
2. Ask questions-problems/need
3. Confirm desire to solve problem
4. Features, benefits, proof
5. Trial close

HANDLING OBJECTIONS

CLOSING THE SALE

Objectives of the Presentation

The objective of the Securing Desire section of your presentation is to persuade your prospect to want to buy your product or service. Since you are to assume he or she has never done business with your firm, you must first provide some information about the firm. Then you will discover the prospect's problems and needs, while providing the benefits of your product or service and of doing business with you and your company. When the prospect seems skeptical, you will offer proof of the benefits. Appropriate words, visual aids, and audio aids will be used to dramatize the benefits.

Preparing to Secure Desire

Prospect and Consumer Problems and Needs

Since the type of presentation you are developing is called *need satisfaction selling,* the entire presentation revolves around the prospect's needs and problems. The first step in this approach is to identify the prospect's needs. These are gaps between his or her current situation and the ideal situation. General needs of businesses and consumers were discussed in Chapter 5. Refer to pages 31 and 32 and review this discussion. The *specific* needs the prospect might have must be identified in the Securing Desire section. The following are some examples of specific needs a sporting goods buyer and consumer might have related to Fusion. Also, there is an example of needs a sales manager and salespeople might have related to a sales training workshop. The workshop is being sold by a marketing consulting firm to a sales manager who is considering a training program for her sales representatives.

FUSION RUNNING SHOES
Problems/needs of the athletic shoe buyer

1. Increase sales, profits, and turnover
2. Offer high-quality products that satisfy consumer needs
3. Buy from a dependable company, which has knowledgeable, service-oriented salespeople
4. Generate more store traffic
5. Receive advertising support and promotional discounts

Problems/needs of the consumer

1. Improve running performance
2. Have greater comfort
3. Reduce foot, ankle, and knee injuries
4. Enjoy running more
5. Improve health, fitness, and sex appeal
6. Receive good value in relation to price

SALES TRAINING WORKSHOP
Problems/needs of the sales manager

1. Increase company sales and profits
2. Improve effectiveness of sales training
3. Reduce time and cost to train sales representatives
4. Provide a comprehensive training program relevant for both new and veteran salespeople

Problems/needs of the workshop participants (salespeople)

1. Increase territory sales and personal income
2. Gain hands-on knowledge of successful selling techniques
3. Experience an exciting presentation of workshop material
4. Improve management of time resulting in more leisure time with family and friends

---

Features, Advantages, and Benefits

Once the prospect problems and needs have been identified, you can present the features, advantages, and benefits related to the problems and needs.

Features—physical characteristics of a company or product, or description of a service. Features are facts about your company, product, or service. They may be tangible, such as the materials your product is made of, including size, color, or shape. Examples of intangible features are fast delivery, knowledgeable service personnel, and technical support. Features answer the prospect's question "What is it?"

Advantages—what the features will do. If a feature of a product is that it is made of stainless steel, the advantage is that it will not rust.

Benefits—favorable results the prospect will enjoy from the features. Benefits are derived from features and explain what the features do for the prospect. They relate features to the prospect and answer the question "What's in it for me?" People are motivated to buy based on benefits, not features, so you should mention features in your presentation, but stress the benefits.

One technique to help you distinguish among feature, advantage, and benefit statements is to try to put them in the following sentence.

This has . . . (feature) . . . so that . . . (advantage) . . . , which means you . . . (benefit) . . .

"This has *stainless steel parts* so that *it will not rust*, which means you *reduce replacement cost and save money*."

Another test to determine whether something is a feature or a benefit is to challenge the statement with a series of questions that ask "So what?"

This product is advertised on national television. "So what?"

It will have a high rate of turnover in your retail store. "So what?"

You will experience high sales and profits.
(This is the benefit).

Many trainers use the acronym "FAB" to help salespeople remember to present *Features*, *Advantages*, and *Benefits*. "FAB" will be used throughout this text.

The following are some examples of features, advantages, and benefits for Fusion. More examples are on pages 133 and 134. Note how the features and benefits correspond with the problems and needs discussed earlier.

FUSION RUNNING SHOES

Features	Advantages	Benefits
Athletic shoe buyer		
1. The suggested retail price for Fusion is $124.95 with a markup of 46 percent.	The profit margin per unit is $57.95.	The dealer will increase athletic shoe profits.
2. The introductory promotional campaign includes national advertising, point-of-sale material, and brochures.	Consumer awareness of the product will be created.	Store traffic, sales, and profits will be maximized.
3. Brooks has a 10-point quality control inspection procedure.	Defective shoes are identified before they are shipped to the dealer.	The dealer is guaranteed to get high-quality products. Customers will be satisfied.
Consumer		
1. Fusion has a carbon-fiber Propulsion Plate System.	Upon impact, the energy stored in the front of the Propulsion Plate System is released to propel the runner into the next stride.	The performance of the runner is improved so he or she can run faster, with less exertion.

(continued)

FUSION RUNNING SHOES *(continued)*

Features	Advantages	Benefits
Consumer		
2. A dual-chamber HydroFlow pad is in the heel of the shoe.	Shocks from running are absorbed in the shoe rather than by the body.	Foot, ankle, and knee injuries are reduced.
3. Fusion offers an anatomically correct fit in sizes 7 through 13.	The shoe fits better.	The runner can run longer distances with fewer foot abrasions. Health will improve. The shoe feels comfortable, making running more fun.
4. The upper portion of the shoe is white, gray, purple, and orange, and made out of nylon fabric and leather.	Fusion looks attractive and will last longer.	The runner will have more sex appeal and save money in the long run.
5. Fusion has a 30-day, money-back guarantee.	Defective shoes can be returned to the dealer for a full refund.	The consumer is assured he or she won't lose money.

The following are examples of features, advantages, and benefits of a sales training workshop.

SALES TRAINING WORKSHOP

Features	Advantages	Benefits
Sales manager		
1. Over 3,000 salespeople from 400 companies have completed the workshop.	The concepts and methods have been tested and refined, so the training is state-of-the-art.	You are guaranteed to get results in increased sales and profits.
2. The workshop begins with a skills assessment of each participant.	Salesperson strengths and weaknesses are identified.	The training will be effective, since it focuses on overcoming weaknesses. Both new and veteran salespeople will benefit.
3. Topics in the two-day workshop include: —effective prospecting and qualifying methods, —opening a sales call, —determining buyer needs, —handling objections, —closing and follow-up skills, —time and territory management.	Salespeople will gain a comprehensive understanding of all the important skills related to their jobs.	Additional training will not be needed for some time. You will therefore save training time and money.

SALES TRAINING WORKSHOP *(continued)*

Features	Advantages	Benefits
Workshop participant (salespeople)		
1. Participants develop and role play sales presentations on their specific products or services.	Ensures concepts are used properly. Training is hands-on.	Salespeople will conduct more effective presentations resulting in higher territory sales and personal income.
2. Films, case histories, and simulations are used throughout the workshop.	The interest and attention levels will be high.	Participants will learn and retain more.
3. The workshop includes a module on time and territory management.	Participants learn how to save time and maximize productivity.	Salespeople will complete more work, providing leisure time for family, friends, and fun.

We said earlier that the process of persuading a prospect to want to buy your product or service involves first identifying the prospect's needs, then matching those needs to appropriate features and benefits. You may have 10 to 20 features and benefits, but only a few may match a particular prospect's needs. The following figure illustrates a situation in which the prospect has four specific needs, but the salesperson has 16 features and benefits she could present. Rather than overwhelming the prospect with a discussion of all 16 benefits, he or she should present only those related to the needs. Remember, your mission during a presentation is to appeal to this prospect's *specific* buying motives, not to impress him or her with how much you know about your company and product.

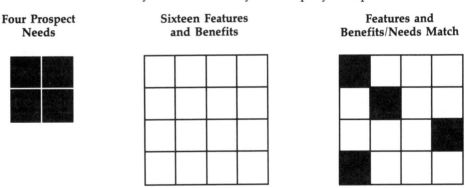

| **Four Prospect Needs** | **Sixteen Features and Benefits** | **Features and Benefits/Needs Match** |

Proving Benefits

A prospect is typically skeptical of a salesperson's claims about the benefits of the product or service, especially if the prospect does not know the salesperson. Therefore, you must provide proof to build trust and convince the prospect that what you say is true. The following are some types of proof.

Company-supplied proof, such as Research and Development Department reports, product or user tests, marketing research studies, company specification sheets, guarantees, warrantees, sales data on your company and product or service, and a list of current customers.

Independent research findings from marketing research firms, articles published in trade journals and newspapers, government agencies, *Consumer Reports* ratings, and Underwriters' Laboratories test results.

Testimonial letters from satisfied customers. When you present these letters, first establish the credibility of the authors. Quote some of the important sections of the letters. Finally, relate this customer's situation to that of this prospect.

Endorsements from experts or prominent people, such as a nationally known physician who recommends a diet food or Michael Jordan who wears Nike basketball shoes.

Case history, which is a story about another company that had good results from using your product or service. Discuss who, what, when, where, how, and any other specific details of the successful results.

Demonstration, such as encouraging a prospect to taste and smell a food product, to sit in an office chair being sold, to type on a word processor, or to accept a free trial offer of a product or service.

This listing is in increasing order of believability. Company-supplied proof is the least convincing, a demonstration the most convincing. If you are selling a product that can be demonstrated, do so. Suggestions on how to conduct a demonstration are on pages 55 and 56.

Dramatization

We have already identified *what* information should be communicated in the body of a presentation—the features, advantages, benefits, and proof that support the prospect's needs. This section deals with *how* to effectively communicate this information.

Prospects have many distractions and time pressures during their workday. A sales representative is competing with other sales representatives, supervisors, secretaries, the telephone, meetings, deadlines, and other distractions. To get and hold a prospect's interest and attention, you must use dramatization techniques and effectively engage as many of the prospect's five senses—hearing, sight, touch, taste, and smell—as possible. Dramatization involves communicating features, benefits, and proof in an attention-getting manner.

Engaging the Sense of Hearing—About 15 percent of all information our minds take in is through our sense of hearing. You must creatively use words, your voice, and sound elements to make your sales presentation stand out.

A sales representative should make a conscious effort to develop a new vocabulary. Every industry has its own jargon. You have to learn it and use it. You should also use special "power words" that will dramatize what you have to say. The prospect's name is the most powerful word you can use. Here is a list of power words to consider:

Prospect's name	Up-to-date	Durable
You, your	Save	Cost-effective
New	Guaranteed*	Quality
Proven*	Economical	Outstanding
Exciting	Easy to use	Value
Successful	State-of-the-art	Engineered
Time-saving	Innovative	Improved
Labor-saving	Recommended*	Efficient
Profits	Tested, safe*	Free

*Excellent words for proof statements

Picture words attempt to paint visual pictures. They translate words into mental images and can dramatically improve your ability to convey features and benefits. The following are some examples:

"Our company is as solid as the Rock of Gibraltar."

"The Propulsion Plate in the sole of this running shoe is like a pole vaulter's pole that will propel you forward."

"The handle of this carving knife is made out of a special, indestructible polyurethane resin, which is the same material of which bowling balls are made."

"Picture yourself driving this sports car down the highway on a warm, sunny day with the top down."

Some words and phrases should be avoided. They can convey incorrect meanings, or they could intimidate or annoy the prospect. Avoid using:

"Sell you." Replace with "Show you how you can benefit."

"Cheap." Use "inexpensive" or "requiring a small investment."

"You pay." Consider "your investment."

"Deal." Use "special offer."

"Contract" in reference to the order form. Replace with "agreement" or "paperwork."

"Sign the order." Use "approve the paperwork."

"Maybe" or "perhaps." These words suggest uncertainty.

"And-uh," "umh," "ya know," and the excessive use of "like."

So far we have discussed power words, picture words, and words to avoid during your sales presentation. While your choice of words is very important in activating the sense of hearing, how you communicate them is equally important. Do not speak in a monotone. Vary your rate of speaking, so it is sometimes fast and at other times slow and deliberate. Vary the volume and always speak enthusiastically.

In addition to words, you can use audio aids to engage the prospect's sense of hearing, such as an audio tape of a radio or television commercial. These can be very effective.

Silence can also be an effective tool in selling. Some sales representatives feel very uncomfortable when either they or the prospect is not talking, but silence is appropriate when you are giving the prospect time to think or reach a decision.

Engaging the Sense of Sight About 77 percent of the information our minds take in is through our sense of sight. Therefore, your sales presentation should be primarily visual, and you should use words to reinforce the visual stimuli. Research has shown that after three days, people remembered approximately six times more information when a presentation involved both visual *and* auditory stimuli than when it involved only auditory stimuli. So show and tell your story, do not just tell it. The following are some examples of how visual aids can be used to communicate benefits or offer proof.

A **portfolio** is anything listed next that can be put in a loose-leaf binder, including price lists and order forms.

Flip chart of the features and benefits of the business telephone system you are selling and a list of the steps to have it installed.

Chart or graph showing the week-by-week reduction of the blood pressure of executives who were participating in your health club's fitness program.

Print ad for your stereo receiver cut out of a consumer magazine to prove you are conducting a heavy advertising campaign. A layout of an ad could be used if the campaign has not started yet. A **storyboard** of your television commercial could be used, too.

Product sample of a racquetball racquet you are selling to the manager of a racquetball club.

Scale model of a solar heating panel to demonstrate to a homeowner how effective silicone chips are in converting sunlight to heat.

Cross section of a steel-belted radial tire to show its features to a distributor.

List of customers who are currently using your security surveillance systems to prove your company is a large and reputable one.

Testimonial letters from sales managers who have used your hotel for sales meetings and have been pleased with your services.

Photographs of a homeowner's yard before and after landscaping.

Catalog of the university you work for to show to high school counselors.

Brochure of the brand of aluminum siding your firm installs.

Slides of the tourist attractions someone will see on the group tour of Europe your travel agency offers.

Videotape (or film) of a television commercial.

Drawing of how new office partitions could be arranged to maximize utilization of space in an office.

Warranty or guarantee statement for a videocassette recorder, indicating that the cost of all parts and labor will be paid for by your company for one year after purchase.

Poster of a sports celebrity who endorses your tennis shoes.

Annual report showing the dramatic growth in sales and profits your company has enjoyed in recent years.

Scratch pad used to write down pricing or a payout plan for your product.

Price sheet and order form.

Test market data showing that your cosmetic product captured a 25 percent share of the market.

Typewritten list of the services your bank offers.

Point-of-sale material used in hardware stores to promote your line of chain saws.

Article that appeared in *U.S. News and World Report* that states your company is a leader in its industry.

Some people who sell services do not use an adequate number of visual aids to make an effective presentation. They feel that since they are selling something intangible, relevant visual aids cannot be developed, so they simply tell their story. However, using visual aids is even more important when selling services than when selling tangible products, because prospects cannot actually see what they are buying. An example will help illustrate the types of visual aids that can be used to sell a service. A salesperson for a firm such as Manpower or Kelly Services, which offers a service of temporary employees to businesses, could use the following visual aids:

Chart listing the features and benefits of hiring temporary rather than permanent workers.

Graph depicting the tremendous growth in the use of temporary workers in recent years.

List of customers the firm provides temporary help to in the local area.

Testimonial letters from satisfied customers and temporary employees of the firm.

Photographs of the exterior of the office building, executives of the firm, and temporary employees in a work setting.

Brochure listing the different types of temporary employees the firm provides, including secretaries, bookkeepers, and data-entry clerks.

Annual report showing the growth in sales of the firm.

Article, which appeared in the local newspaper profiling the firm and its president.

Typewritten list of the step-by-step process used to screen, train, and evaluate new temporary workers.

Sample of the application form prospective temporary workers are required to complete before being hired.

List of the questions used during interviews of prospective temporary employees.

Description of the training the firm offers its temporary workers.

Sample of the form used by supervisors to evaluate temporary workers after they have completed an assignment.

Price sheet detailing the hourly rate the firm charges for different classifications of temporary workers.

Contract the customer signs when hiring temporary workers.

As you can see, the opportunities to use visual aids to sell a service are as numerous as those for selling a product. So show *and* tell the story about your service, do not just tell the story.

There are some additional considerations when using visual aids. Always maintain control of each visual aid. For example, do not give the prospect your brochure to page through at his or her own pace. Place it on the prospect's desk and go through it using your finger and eye movements to direct attention where you want it. Turn pages carefully rather than flipping them, and never put a visual aid or sample back in your attaché case until you have completed the closing sequence. You may need it to handle an objection.

If you are sitting on the opposite side of the prospect's desk, you will have to be able to read printed material upside down. Be familiar with where everything is. Put paper clips on important pages so you can find them quickly. Use a colored marker to highlight important words or phrases.

In all probability, the company you are selling for has few, if any, visual aids for you to use. If this is the case, your sales manager may let you make your own. For example, develop a couple of testimonial letters, sketch something you would like photographed, or construct a graph of test data.

Perhaps the most important visual aid a salesperson has is his or her own physical appearance. A sales representative should be well groomed and dressed appropriately for the product or service being sold and the prospect. The representative should use proper nonverbal communications such as hand gestures, facial expressions, and body positions.

Engaging the Senses of Touch, Smell, and Taste—About 8 percent of the information our minds take in is through our senses of touch, smell, and taste. While this percentage is small compared to that for our sense of sight, these senses should not be overlooked.

Propelled into the Future...

Fusion: A blending, a coalition. The future has arrived with the Brooks Fusion. The Fusion is the alternative in athletic shoes, combining the cushioning features of HydroFlow™ with the performance enhancement technology of the Brooks Propulsion Plate.

The benefit of the Propulsion Plate is that it works throughout the three phases of forward motion: heel strike, midstance, and toe-off. The stability component and external arch support function together to provide smooth transitions from phase one through phase three.

The plate design incorporates a rearfoot stability component, an external arch support, and a forefoot propulsion component that complement the natural spring mechanism of the foot.

The profile of this design is engineered to work synergistically with muscle function and improve biomechanical efficiency for the athlete.

In running, an athlete experiences two load peaks. The first is upon initial foot impact. The second is associated with foot propulsion as the heel is lifted off the ground and the load is shifted to the metatarsal heads of the forefoot.

With the Brooks Propulsion Plate, the velocity and degree of pronation are controlled, while shock is attenuated and potential energy is stored by the external arch support. As the heel is lifted off the ground, the energy is released from the external arch support and assists in bending the forefoot Propulsion Plate as the load is transferred to the metatarsal heads. Throughout the toe-off phase, the energy stored in the forefoot plate is released to provide propulsion into the next stride.

These advancements in the Midsole Concept are further evidence of Brooks' commitment to developing technologically advanced, anatomically correct athletic footwear.

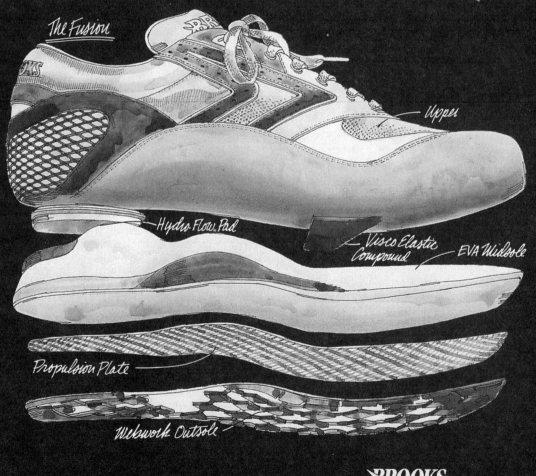

The Fusion — Upper — Hydro-Flow Pad — Visco Elastic Compound — EVA Midsole — Propulsion Plate — Webwork Outsole

≫BROOKS
It's all in the shoes.

The sense of touch can be engaged by something as simple as shaking the prospect's hand when you greet and say good-bye. Physical touching in this socially acceptable way begins to break down the barriers between salesperson and prospect and to facilitate establishing a rapport.

Another means of engaging this sense is handing something to the prospect, such as a sample of your product. Have him or her hold and examine it. People like to touch and feel things they buy. If you conduct a demonstration, have the prospect do it while you direct what to do.

The sense of smell can be engaged if you are demonstrating a food or cosmetic product. If you are discussing the fragrance of something, you should smell it first and then have the prospect smell it. Describe the fragrance using words that are as descriptive as possible. Salespeople with bad breath and body odor can engage this sense in a negative manner.

Our sense of taste is closely associated with our sense of smell. If you are doing a taste test, have a sample of the product for you and one for the prospect. You should smell and then taste your sample while the prospect does so with the other sample. Describe the fragrance and taste using descriptive words that emphasize the product's features and benefits.

Conducting a Demonstration—Earlier we mentioned that a demonstration is the most effective way to dramatize features and benefits. It is effective, because it allows the prospect to see that the product is a good one. It also allows the salesperson to engage the prospect's senses of hearing, sight, touch, taste, and smell. The following are some examples of how a demonstration could be used to communicate benefits.

Product	Benefit	Demonstration
Office chair	Comfort	Ask the prospect to sit in the chair
Wine	Good taste and bouquet	Offer the prospect the opportunity to smell and taste the wine
Facsimile machine	Ease of installing the machine and transmitting documents	Have the prospect install the machine and transmit a document while you are instructing on what to do
Word processing software	Ease of use	Let the prospect perform some routine word processing functions
Expensive set of carving knives	Sharpness and ease of cutting	Give the prospect a fresh tomato and ask him or her to cut it

There are several points to consider when conducting a demonstration.

A. Plan the demonstration—Determine what features and benefits will be communicated and what material will be needed. Consider the setting of where the demonstration will be conducted, and make sure things like electrical outlets and a table are available if needed.

B. Practice, practice, practice—The best way to lose a sale is to have the demonstration not go smoothly. You do not want to fumble around or give the impression that you do not know how the product is supposed to operate.

C. Anticipate problems—List all the things that could go wrong and know how to correct them.

D. Get the prospect physically and mentally involved. Have him or her actively participate, and ask questions to solicit favorable comments.

E. Identify the prospect's needs, problems, and concerns. Address them with your features and benefits during the demonstration.

Some products such as computers or photocopy machines require a demonstration, but are too large to bring to the prospect's office. If your company has them on display in a showroom, consider asking the prospect to accompany you to the showroom. Very large products, such as stamping or robotic machines, may require you to take the prospect to a customer's place of business to see the product in operation.

Features-Benefits Worksheet

It's time to begin applying the concepts you have learned about Securing Desire. On pages 135 and 136 is a worksheet to help you identify the features, benefits, proof, and dramatization to use during your presentation. The one provided on pages 133 and 134 is for Fusion and should be a good model for yours. Note that the worksheets fold out to an 11" × 16" size and that they have two sides.

First, identify your prospect's problems/needs and those of the ultimate consumer if the consumer is involved. Selling a product such as jeans to a retail store requires you to identify the problems/needs of the retailer and the consumer. If you are selling an industrial product such as cleaning solvents to a manufacturing firm, you are concerned only with the company needs. In the case of selling a service such as solar heating to a homeowner, only the consumer's problems/needs must be identified. Be sure that for every problem/need you identify you have one or more benefits that will solve the problem or satisfy the need.

Features and benefits can be found in the following areas:

1. The industry your company participates in

2. Your company

3. Your product or service

4. Your product or service's price

5. Your company's distribution and delivery system

6. Your company's promotional programs

Remember, if you are selling something that will be resold, such as a brand of golf clubs to a pro shop, profit is usually the major benefit.

Fill out the worksheet on pages 135 and 136 in number 2 pencil so you can make changes and leave room to add to your list later. Often when you identify objections, you must come up with additional benefits and features to resolve them.

Steps in Securing Desire

Step 1. Familiarize the Prospect with Your Company

Since you are assuming the prospect has never done business with your company before, you must provide him or her with an overview of the company and explain why it is uniquely qualified to serve the prospect's needs. Begin by asking what the prospect already knows about your company. Then provide the following information:

1. A brief history of the firm—Tell a story about when your company was founded and by whom. If photographs of the original building or founders are available, share them with the prospect. Discuss how the company has changed.

2. Major achievements in recent years—These might include the introduction of innovative products or services, awards the company received, acquisitions, or expansions. Consider showing the prospect a chronological list of these achievements.

3. Size in terms of sales, number of employees, or number of locations—If your firm is an industry leader, convey this to the prospect. People like to do business with large reputable firms with a proven track record. Show the prospect a copy of your firm's annual report and discuss its growth in sales. If your firm is small, stress the benefits of being small, such as personalized service and quick response to customer requests. Provide photographs of the executives accompanied by a brief biography of each. Discuss the experience they have had.

4. Types of products or services you offer—Show the prospect a brochure or typewritten list of the broad range of products or services you offer.

5. List of current customers—Be sure to include large firms that buy from you and, ideally, those that compete directly or indirectly with the prospect.

The purpose of this step is to establish the credibility of your firm and to convince the prospect it is worthwhile to do business with it. This discussion should be from 30 seconds to one minute in length and should include one or two visual aids.

Step 2. Ask Need-Discovery Questions Until You Identify a Specific Problem

In Step 5 of the Approach you asked fact-finding questions to determine the prospect's current situation. Now you must continue to question the prospect until one problem or need is identified. You will recall that problems or needs are gaps between the prospect's current situation and the ideal situation. These questions should allow you to diagnose the prospect, just as a doctor diagnoses patients. Identify the ailment. Guide the prospect through the use of questions to identify a problem or need, concerning which your product or service enjoys a competitive advantage. Identifying these problems is the most challenging part of Securing Desire. Start with general, open-ended questions to see if the prospect has any in mind.

"What problems have you been having?"

"How would you describe the ideal situation?"

"Exactly what are you looking for?"

If the prospect offers some problems, ask him or her to elaborate on them. Find out all the details.

"Tell me more."

"Could you elaborate on that point?"

"What do you mean by _____?"

Often, the prospect does not have a clear understanding of problems or needs. In this case, offer some specific ones with closed questions.

"Do you ever get complaints about _____?"

"Have you experienced problems in the area of _____?"

"Are you totally satisfied with _____?"

"Does _____ meet your needs?"

"Is _____ a concern of yours?"

Refer to your completed Features-Benefits Worksheet on pages 135 and 136. The problems and needs should be noted on the top portion of the form.

It is important for you to understand that the fact-finding questions in the Approach are different from the need-discovery questions in the Securing Desire section. The example used in the Approach was that of a salesperson selling health club memberships for executives. The following questions will demonstrate the difference.

Fact-Finding Questions—Step 5 of the Approach

"How many employees work for this company?"

"How many are considered middle or upper management?"

"Do you currently have a fitness program for executives?"

"Have you talked to any other health clubs that offer executive fitness programs?"

"Does your company pay health insurance premiums for your executives?"

Need-Discovery Questions—Step 2 of Securing Desire

"What role do you think physical fitness plays in a person's health and well-being?"

"What kinds of health concerns do some of your managers have, such as smoking, excessive weight, backaches, high blood pressure, or high cholesterol levels?"

"Are some of your managers under a lot of stress? How do you think this affects their performance?"

"Do you find that the health insurance premiums for your executives are increasing? If so, by how much?"

The first problem/need you identify should be one that provides an opportunity to discuss the most important features and benefits of your product or service. You must show your product or explain the details of your service. After the prospect fully understands what is being sold, other needs can be exploited.

The examples that follow illustrate features and benefits related to three problems/needs for different products and services. Notice that, in each case, the first one allows the salesperson to show the product or explain the details of the service.

Product or service being sold	Identify problems/needs related to the . . .
Running shoe sold to a retail sporting goods buyer	1. features and benefits of the running shoe 2. details of the advertising and promotional program 3. profits the retailer will enjoy
Industrial cleaning solvent sold to a manufacturing firm	1. chemical composition of the product and why it cleans floors so well 2. ease of application and use 3. savings of time and money to clean floors

Product or service being sold	Identify problems/needs related to the . . .
Hotel meeting rooms sold to a sales manager planning a training program	1. size of the meeting rooms, seating arrangements, and audiovisual equipment available 2. variety and quality of the food served to guests 3. overnight guest rooms and accommodations
Radio station advertising time sold to a local retailer	1. type of music, news, weather, and sports programming 2. efficiency of the station in reaching the retailer's target audience 3. capabilities of station personnel to write and produce a radio commercial for the retailer

Questions to determine all of the prospect's problems/needs should not be asked one after another. Ask questions to identify *one* problem/need and support it with features, benefits, and proof. Then ask additional questions to identify a *second* problem/need and support it with features, benefits, and proof.

Step 3. Confirm the Prospect's Desire to Solve the Problem or Satisfy the Need

Here you are trying to "pin the prospect down" and get him or her to agree that there is a problem or need. If you cannot get the prospect to agree to this, nothing will be bought.

To confirm the prospect's desire, the following types of questions can be asked.

"Then you're looking for _____?"

"So you need a way to _____?"

"Can I assume a solution to that problem would be of interest to you?"

"You want _____?"

"Is solving that problem a concern of yours?"

"If I could show you a plan that would _____, would you be interested?"

Step 4. Provide Features, Benefits, and Proof that Will Solve the Problem or Satisfy the Need—Use Dramatization

Step 3 got the prospect to agree there was a problem/need. Step 4 must show the prospect that (1) he or she has a need for the *type* of product/service you are offering, (2) your specific *brand* of product will meet these needs, (3) your *company* is worth doing business with, (4) your *price* is right, and (5) now is the *time* to buy.

The information used to convince the prospect that you can solve a problem includes the features, advantages, benefits, proof, and dramatization discussed earlier. Consider using the acronym "FAB+PD" to remember what to say and how to say it. "Gobble up" the prospect's problems and needs using FAB + PD.

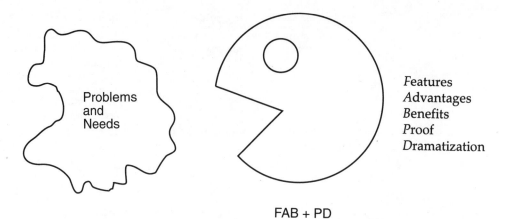

Problems and Needs

Features
Advantages
Benefits
Proof
Dramatization

FAB + PD

Refer to your completed Features-Benefits Worksheet on pages 135 and 136 for your FAB + PD. Also, refer to the discussion on dramatization beginning on page 50. Use appropriate words, audio aids, and visual aids. Engage the prospect's senses of sight, hearing, touch, smell, and taste. Do a demonstration, if appropriate.

The issue of whether you should mention competitor products or services when you are discussing features and benefits is controversial. It is usually best not to mention competitors unless the prospect brings it up, or unless it is absolutely necessary. If you do mention them, be professional. Do not speak disparagingly about competitors. Rather, you might show how their products are good, but yours is better.

Step 5. Offer a Trial Close

You will learn in the section on Closing that you should close the sale when the prospect is ready to close. This may be before you have presented all your benefits. To determine whether the prospect is ready to close, you must frequently ask questions to get a reaction or opinion on something you have said. These are called trial closes, and they give the prospect an opportunity to give you a buying signal. They are opinion-seeking questions, not order-asking questions. Trial close questions test the prospect's readiness to buy. They are designed to measure the prospect's buying "temperature: cold, warm, or hot." Ask trial close questions after presenting important benefits or after attempting to resolve an objection. If the answer to your question is positive, you may wish to ask a closing question and close the sale. Here are some examples of trial closes you can use in the body of the presentation:

"What's your reaction to what I've said so far?"

"How does that sound?"

"What do you think?"

"That's great, isn't it?"

"You *would* like to (state benefit), wouldn't you?"

"Is this what you're looking for?"

"In your opinion, do you feel this is an important benefit?"

"How does that strike you?"

"Does that make sense?"

"Am I on the right track?"

Step 6. Close or Repeat Steps 2 through 5

After the trial close, if you sense the prospect is ready to agree to buy, ask for the order. If not, repeat Steps 2, 3, 4, and 5. Identify another problem, confirm the desire to solve the problem, provide features, benefits, and proof, then ask another trial close question. Refer to the diagram on the inside front cover. Notice the arrows that show how to recycle the steps in Securing Desire or to proceed to Closing the Sale.

Example of Securing Desire

The following is an example of the Securing Desire section of the presentation for Fusion. It begins where the Approach section left off. Recall that Jeff Dykehouse is conducting a presentation with Penny Taylor, the buyer at a sporting goods store. Review the Fusion example beginning on page 35 before you read the next section.

PLANNING GUIDE—FUSION SECURING DESIRE

Salesperson-Prospect Dialogue

Step 1. Familiarize the prospect with information about your company he or she does not already have.

SALESPERSON: *Penny, do you know very much about Brooks?*

PROSPECT: *Not really. I know Brooks has been around for a long time, and I've seen some of your ads in* Runner's World.

SALESPERSON: *Brooks got started back in 1914, so we have been in the shoe business for a long time. In 1972, we began to produce our own brand of athletic shoes. Our corporate headquarters are located in Rockford, Michigan.*

While we concentrate our efforts on running and walking shoes, we offer a full line of athletic shoes. (Show "Footwear Catalog." Point out the categories of shoes we sell.)

Brooks is the official shoe company for the Ironman World Triathlon Championships in Hawaii and the Coors Lite Biathlon series. Also, we have the only running shoe technology that is endorsed by the American Podiatric Medical Association. (Show certificate that verifies this endorsement.)

Our line is very well established in the west Michigan area. (Show the list of customers. Mention some.)

Pretty impressive isn't it?

PROSPECT: *Yes it is.*

SALESPERSON: *We offer high-quality products that will provide handsome profits for your store, Penny.*

PLANNING GUIDE—FUSION SECURING DESIRE *(continued)*

Salesperson-Prospect Dialogue

Step 2. Question(s) to identify first problem/need

SALESPERSON: *What would you say your customers look for in the running shoes they buy?*

PROSPECT: *A shoe has to look good, but most of my customers are looking for a shoe that will provide better performance and reduce injuries.*

Step 3. Question to confirm prospect's desire to solve problem or satisfy first need

SALESPERSON: *If I could show you a product that will offer your customers these benefits, would you be interested?*

PROSPECT: *Yes.*

Step 4. Features/benefits/proof to support first problem/need. Use dramatization.

SALESPERSON: *Penny, here it is. (Show sample. Get reaction.) Fusion is the most technologically advanced shoe in the industry. What makes it so unique is the carbon fiber Propulsion Plate System in the midsole. (Give Penny the Propulsion Plate sample.) The way it works is, upon impact, the energy stored in the front of the Plate is released to propel the runner into the next stride. (Do a demonstration with the Plate.) It acts like a pole vaulter's pole. The energy stored in the pole propels the vaulter over the bar. The shoe's structure allows it to similarly store energy. The benefit is that the runner's speed and endurance are enhanced.*

Fusion also contains the patented HydroFlow pad in the heel of the shoe. (Show example.) The tremendous impact on the foot while running cushions like a shock absorber. (Do a demonstration.) This will help reduce foot injuries.

Both of these technologies were developed by the Biomechanics Evaluation Laboratory at Michigan State University. (Show B.E.L. brochure. Discuss research activities.) Fusion is available in men's and women's sizes.

Step 5. Trial close

SALESPERSON: *What do you think, Penny?*

PROSPECT: *It sounds good so far.*

PLANNING GUIDE—FUSION SECURING DESIRE *(continued)*

Salesperson-Prospect Dialogue

Step 2. Question(s) to identify second problem/need

SALESPERSON: *This is a relatively new store, Penny. Are you satisfied with the amount of traffic you are getting?*

PROSPECT: *We had a good Christmas season, but it is dead right now. You know what Michigan winters are like.*

Step 3. Question to confirm prospect's desire to solve problem or satisfy second need

SALESPERSON: *So you need a way to get more shoppers in your store?*

PROSPECT: *That would be nice.*

Step 4. Features/benefits/proof to support second problem/need. Use dramatization.

SALESPERSON: *We have developed an extensive promotional campaign for Fusion that will create awareness of the product in your trading area and bring customers into your store.*

Our four-color, two-page spreads will begin in the April editions of Runner's World *and* Running Times. *The ads will also appear in* Michigan Runner. *(Show samples of ads.) We produced a nine-minute videotape that will air on the ''Health and Fitness Today'' show. We also have an excellent co-op advertising program. (Show ''Co-op Advertising Planner'' booklet. Discuss details.)*

At the point of sale there are display units, posters, and brochures available that tie in with our advertising. (Show samples.)

Finally, we have world-class atheletes, such as runners like Bill Rogers, triathletes like Paula Newby-Fraser and Dave Scott, who will be endorsing the Brooks line this season. (Quote from the ads that feature testimonials from these runners.)

Step 5. Trial close

SALESPERSON: *How does that sound?*

PROSPECT: *It's impressive. But what is the retail price of the shoe? (Address price in the profit benefit.)*

PLANNING GUIDE—FUSION SECURING DESIRE *(continued)*

Salesperson-Prospect Dialogue

Step 2. Question(s) to identify third problem/need

SALESPERSON: *This is a beautiful store in a prime location. Your overhead must be pretty high. Penny, do you find it more and more difficult to turn a profit?*

PROSPECT: *That's an understatement!*

Step 3. Question to confirm prospect's desire to solve third problem or satisfy third need

SALESPERSON: *Then you want to maximize your profit margin and profit per unit on your running shoes?*

PROSPECT: *Isn't that what being in business is all about?*

Step 4. Features/benefits/proof to support third problem/need. Use dramatization.

SALESPERSON: *Take a look at our profit schedule on Fusion. I think you'll be impressed. (Show visual aid that details pricing and profits.)*

As you can see, our suggested retail price on Fusion is $124.95. Your investment is $67.00 per pair so you make $57.95 profit on each unit sold. That's 46 percent!

Now, if you turn only four pairs per week, that's $231.80 in profits. If you compare this to the profits you make on an $80 shoe, we're 60 percent higher. With our heavy advertising, you could easily turn 30 to 40 pairs this season. That would mean $1,500 to $2,000 profits just on Fusion!

Step 5. Trial close

SALESPERSON: *Is this the kind of profit you're looking for, Penny?*

PROSPECT: *Yes, it is in line with our expectations.*

Preparing to Role Play

Planning Guide Form—Securing Desire

You can now apply the principles you have learned about Securing Desire to your own product or service. Refer to your completed Features-Benefits Worksheet on pages 135 and 136 for the needs, features, benefits, proof, and dramatization when you complete the Planning Guide that follows. Prepare questions to identify three problems/needs. Provide a complete dialogue of what you and the prospect say. Complete the forms neatly, using a number 2 pencil, so they can be changed and photocopied. Study the rating form on page 72 to make sure you have not forgotten anything.

PLANNING GUIDE—SECURING DESIRE

Salesperson-Prospect Dialogue

Refer to the example of the completed Planning Guide on pages 62 through 65.

Step 1. Familiarize the prospect with information about your company he or she does not already have. *(Fill out this form neatly in number 2 pencil. See pages 56 and 57.)*

PLANNING GUIDE—SECURING DESIRE *(continued)*

Salesperson-Prospect Dialogue

Step 2. Question(s) to identify first problem/need *(The first need should allow you to discuss the most important benefits your product or service has to offer. Also, show your product or explain your service. See pages 57 through 59.)*

Step 3. Question to confirm prospect's desire to solve first problem or satisfy first need *(See page 59.)*

Step 4. Features/benefits/proof to support first problem/need. Use dramatization. *(Refer to your Features-Benefits Worksheet on pages 135 and 136. Also, see pages 59 and 60.)*

Step 5. Trial close *(See page 60.)*

PLANNING GUIDE—SECURING DESIRE *(continued)*

Salesperson-Prospect Dialogue

Step 2. Question(s) to identify second problem/need

Step 3. Question to confirm prospect's desire to solve second problem or satisfy second need

Step 4. Features/benefits/proof to support second problem/need. Use dramatization.

Step 5. Trial close *(Use a different trial close than for the first problem/need.)*

PLANNING GUIDE—SECURING DESIRE *(continued)*

Salesperson-Prospect Dialogue

Step 2. Question(s) to identify third problem/need

Step 3. Question to confirm prospect's desire to solve third problem or satisfy third need

Step 4. Features/benefits/proof to support third problem/need. Use dramatization.

Step 5. Trial close *(Use a different trial close than for the first two problems/needs.)*

(PROSPECT: At some point during the Securing Desire section of the presentation, you should ask about the price of the product or service.)

How the Role Play Will Be Conducted

Your sales manager may have you role play Securing Desire. If not, you can role play it on your own or get two other people to participate. Review the instructions in the section "How the Role Play Will Be Conducted" on page 43. This also applies to role playing Securing Desire. You will not role play the Approach. Assuming you have just completed the Approach, you will be seated when you begin. Do not try to close the sale. The prospect should not offer any objections during this role play.

Materials Needed to Role Play Securing Desire

You will need your completed Setting the Scene Form on page 39, Planning Guide, a photocopy of the four-page Planning Guide for the prospect, Securing Desire Rating Form, product samples, visual and audio aids, and *RPPS* manual. If you are going to do a demonstration of your product, you will need the materials for it. If you do not have access to a photocopy machine to reproduce your Planning Guide for the prospect, make a typewritten or handwritten copy of the salesperson-prospect dialogue for Steps 2 and 3, including the titles of the steps.

Securing Desire Rating Form (25 Points)

Salesperson's Company: _____   Hour: _____

Product/Service: _____   Salesperson's Name: _____

Prospect's Company: _____

	Possible Score	Actual Score
		Record Scores of Three Role Plays
—Ability to briefly familiarize the prospect with your company	2	_____ _____ _____
—Ability to ask questions and clearly identify problems/needs	3	_____ _____ _____
—Ability to confirm the prospect's desire to solve each problem or satisfy each need	2	_____ _____ _____
—Ability to provide features and benefits relevant to each problem/need	5	_____ _____ _____
—Ability to offer proof, including a demonstration, if appropriate	3	_____ _____ _____
—Ability to offer a trial close after each benefit statement	2	_____ _____ _____
—Ability to incorporate visual (and/or audio) aids, if appropriate, into the presentation, put them in front of the prospect, and maintain control of them	3	_____ _____ _____
—Ability to use the prospect's name, power words, and picture words	3	_____ _____ _____
—Ability to be an enthusiastic, active listener and to keep the prospect involved	2	_____ _____ _____
Total	25 pts.	_____ _____ _____

Coach's notes and comments:

HANDLING OBJECTIONS

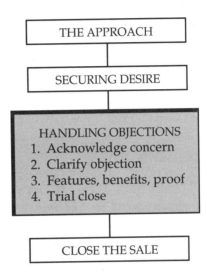

```
┌─────────────────────────────┐
│        THE APPROACH         │
└─────────────────────────────┘
              │
┌─────────────────────────────┐
│       SECURING DESIRE       │
└─────────────────────────────┘
              │
┌─────────────────────────────┐
│     HANDLING OBJECTIONS     │
│  1. Acknowledge concern     │
│  2. Clarify objection       │
│  3. Features, benefits, proof│
│  4. Trial close             │
└─────────────────────────────┘
              │
┌─────────────────────────────┐
│        CLOSE THE SALE       │
└─────────────────────────────┘
```

Goals of Handling Objections

Most of the time when a salesperson tries to close the sale, the prospect has one or more reasons for not wanting to buy. Overcoming this resistance to achieve the sales call objective is called Handling Objections. The prospect needs more justification (benefits) and reassurance (proof) before he or she can make a buying decision.

Preparing to Handle Objections

Anticipating Objections

Throughout this text, the importance of a salesperson being prepared has been stressed. This need to be prepared applies especially to the area of Handling Objections. A salesperson must anticipate the prospect's objections and determine ahead of time what benefits will resolve each one.

No purchase is ever made—whether it is a seventy-five cent candy bar or a $25,000 automobile—unless the prospect says "yes" to five questions, called the Five Buying Decisions. They are:

Question 1. "Do I *need* it?" (e.g., a new car)

Question 2. "Will this *product (or service)* satisfy the need or solve the problem?" (e.g., a Honda Accord)

Question 3. "Is this *source* (company and sales representative) the one from whom I should buy?" (e.g., a specific Honda dealership)

Question 4. "Is the *price* right/*money* available?" (e.g., the sticker price, rebates, trade-in allowances, and financing)

Question 5. "Is the *time* to buy now?"

The salesperson must obtain five affirmative responses before the prospect will buy.

This concept is useful when anticipating objections, because all objections can be classified under one of the Five Buying Decisions. The following are examples of objections for Fusion, which is being sold to a retailer; a cellular car telephone, which is being sold to a service manager; and a sales training workshop, which is being offered to a sales manager. Note that all the objections are classified as need, product/service, source, price/money, or time objections. Also, note that they are declarative statements of the reasons the prospect does not want to buy. Make sure the objections you identify are declarative statements, not questions that request more information (e.g., "Your price is too high," rather than "Can you tell me what your price is?")

Objections for Fusion

Need Objections

"We already stock four brands of running shoes."

"I don't have any room on the shelf for another line."

"We have too much inventory of the brands we stock now."

Product/Service Objections

"I think the features of the Nike 180 Air shoe are better than the Propulsion Plate in your shoe."

"Personally, I prefer the styling of the Nike 180 Air."

Source Objections (objections related to doing business with the salesperson or the salesperson's company)

"Your company isn't spending enough money in advertising to promote this shoe."

"Brooks is a small company compared to Nike and Reebok."

"I like the salesperson from Nike. He has some good merchandising ideas and accepts returns on defective shoes."

Price/Money Objections

"Your suggested retail price of $124.95 is too high. People won't pay that much for a shoe."

"I don't have the money to tie up in another line."

"Your shoe doesn't have a proven track record. I don't think the turnover and profits will be adequate."

Time Objections (objections related to allowing the salesperson to achieve the sales call objective during this sales call)

"I want to postpone a decision until next month."

"There is still snow on the ground. People won't buy running shoes until spring."

Objections for a Cellular Car Phone

Need Objections

"Our technicians can use pay phones when they are out making service calls."

"Calls can be made in the morning before our technicians leave the office or in the late afternoon when they return."

Product/Service Objections

"If our technicians use the phone while driving, they may be more apt to have an accident."

"The other model we are looking at has more features."

"Yours only has a two-year warranty."

Source Objections

"We're negotiating with two other cellular phone companies."

"Your company doesn't have its own service department."

"The last salesperson from your company who called on us was a real jerk."

Price/Money Objections

"The price of this unit is 15 percent higher than the other one we are considering."

"The cost of each call on a cellular phone is very high."

Time Objections

"Call me back in a week or so."

"I have to get approval from my boss."

Objections for a Two-Day Sales Training Workshop

Need Objections

"I don't need your workshop, because my salespeople are already well trained."

"I conducted some training about one year ago."

"All my salespeople have at least five years of experience and are college graduates."

Product/Service Objections

"We think on-the-job training is better."

"Your workshop isn't appropriate for experienced salespeople."

"I think a one-day workshop would be adequate."

Source Objections

"I have never heard of your consulting firm."

"Your workshop leader doesn't have any experience selling the types of products we offer."

"Most of your former clients are manufacturing firms. We are a distributor."

Price/Money Objections

"Your price of $490 for each participant is too high."

"I'll lose money during the two days my salespeople are in the workshop and not out selling."

Time Objections   (Same objections as for the previous cellular car phone example.)

The way to prevent objections is to anticipate them and to build into the Securing Desire section of your presentation benefits that will resolve them before they come up.

How to Resolve Need, Product/Service, and Source Objections

The information needed to resolve objections consists of features, benefits, and proof, which are inherent in your industry, company, product or service, price, distribution system, and promotional programs. Many of the benefits you will need to resolve objections are listed in your Features-Benefits Worksheet on pages 135 and 136.

Need objections are ones related to buying *any product or service* offered by your industry rather than your specific brand of product or type of service. To overcome these objections, provide features and benefits that show the prospect the consequences of not buying. A cellular car phone salesperson might discuss how it can save time, improve the productivity, and improve customer relations.

Product or service objections are those associated with buying *your model of product or type of service.* Resolve these objections by discussing the special features and benefits of the product. Mention how it is made, of what it is made, and how it can be used. Discuss workmanship, durability, and quality. Depending on what you are selling, it might be appropriate to discuss how the product will save time or money. If you are selling a service, provide features and benefits of each aspect of the service and explain why your company's employees are qualified to provide superior service.

Source objections deal with resistance to *doing business with your company or with you personally.* Provide features and benefits to show that your firm is reputable and that it is worthwhile to do business with it. Case histories or testimonial letters from satisfied customers can be very effective. Occasionally, salespeople get source objections, because prospects want to continue to buy from competitor salespeople. Overcome these objections by talking about your formal education, training, expertise, and successes with other customers.

How to Resolve Price/Money Objections

The objections that seem to challenge salespeople the most are price objections. It is one area in which the prospect can make a quantitative comparison between two competing products or services. However, prospects rarely buy based on price alone. If a salesperson anticipates price objections and develops means to resolve them before the sales call, these objectives can be overcome. Here are some methods to consider when handling price objections.

1. Build up the *value* of the product or service—The perceived cost of a product is a function of the value received from its benefits and its price. If the price is high and the value is low, the perceived cost is high. Likewise, if the value received from a purchase is high relative to its price, the perceived cost is low. Consider the following formulas:

$$\frac{\text{Price}}{\textit{Value}} = \text{Cost} \qquad\qquad \frac{\text{Price}}{\textit{Value}} = \textit{Cost}$$

    To increase the perceived value of your product or service, stress its unique features and benefits.

2. Explain the return on investment—Assume a salesperson is selling an expensive photocopy machine. It produces copies 30 percent faster than the com-

petitor's model, but it costs more. The higher price could be justified by calculating the wage savings for the time people spend standing at the machine waiting for copies to be run.

3. Calculate the total cost of ownership over the life of the product—The cost of ownership is made up of the initial price plus the other costs related to its use. A furnace that is 95 percent energy efficient might cost $750 more than one that is 70 percent energy efficient, but the cost of natural gas to heat a home would be substantially less with the first furnace. With the more expensive furnace, calculate the savings in the cost of natural gas over the 20-year life of the furnace and compare it with the $750 higher price.

4. Break down the price to smaller units—The cost of a half-page newspaper advertisement might be $2,000, but it would cost only 2 cents per reader. The price of an automobile could be $20,000 but the monthly payments are only $375.

5. Sell the value added—A higher price could be justified by explaining the value your company adds to the purchase, such as fast delivery, free repair or maintenance service, technical assistance, or extensive consumer advertising and promotional support.

6. Show the prospect a lower-priced model in your line.

7. Prove that a higher-priced option will increase the prospect's profits—A product that costs the consumer more might also provide more margin of profit to the retailer. For example, a videocassette recorder, which costs the consumer $500, might offer the retailer a $200 profit margin, while a $300 model provides only a $90 profit margin.

Whenever you discuss price with the prospect, avoid using such terms as "cheap" or "cheaper." "Cheap" indicates poor quality. Also, replace "cost," with "investment."

How to Resolve Time Objections

Time objections are those related to allowing the salesperson to achieve his or her sales call objective during *this* sales call. The prospect might say, "I want to wait until next week before I decide to buy" or "I have to discuss this matter with my boss." If it is a legitimate time objection, you must provide some compelling reason to buy today rather than waiting. Refer to the Buy Now Method of Closing the Sale on page 99 for examples of how to resolve this objection.

Examples of Resolving Objections

In the Handling Objections Planning Guide on pages 89 through 93, you will be asked to identify five objections to your product or service and provide features, benefits, proof, and dramatization that will resolve each one. The following are examples of how to Handle Objections for a two-day sales training workshop, which is being presented to a sales manager. Examples of how to Handle Objections for Fusion are provided on pages 83 through 87.

TWO-DAY SALES TRAINING WORKSHOP

Type of Objection	Objection	Strategy to Resolve Objection	Dramatization and Proof
Need	"My salespeople don't need your workshop, because they are already well trained."	Ask the sales manager what formal training each salesperson has had. Find out how current it is. Point out that the workshop involves improving skills that are lacking in his or her salespeople.	Show him or her a list of the topics covered in the workshop. Provide some details of each topic. Quote from two testimonial letters written by experienced salespeople who completed the course.
Product/ Service	"We think on-the-job training is more effective."	Compare and contrast the skills that can be developed using on-the-job versus formal training. Point out that a combination of both training methods should be used.	Use the article called "The Advantages and Disadvantages of On-the-Job Sales Training," which appeared in a trade magazine. Provide a diagram of how the two training methods can be integrated.
Source	"I have never heard of your consulting firm."	Provide a brief history of the firm. Discuss the qualifications of its key executives, especially of the person who will conduct the workshop.	Show the prospect a list of some of the firm's clients and an article that appeared in the local newspaper, which praised the firm. Use a photograph of the firm's top executives and workshop leader.
Price/ Money	"Your price of $490 for each participant is too high."	Justify the price based on return on investment.	Share two case histories with the prospect. Point out that these firms experienced a 10 percent increase in sales after completing the workshop.
Time	"Call me back in a week or so."	Use a concession. Point out that if he or she makes a decision right now, you will give each participant a free copy of the book called "Success Stories of the World's Best Salespeople" worth $29 each.	Show the prospect a sample of the book. Discuss the Table of Contents with him or her. Mention some of the people who are profiled in the book.

When to Resolve Objections

Prospects may offer objections at any time during the sales presentation. It is generally advisable to try to resolve them when they arise. Postponement may alienate the prospect. However, if a prospect offers a price objection early in the presentation, before you have had a chance to discuss important features and benefits, it may be advisable to postpone answering it. Assure him or her you will address these concerns after you have explained more details about the product or service.

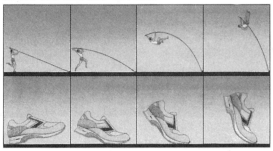

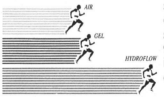

Steps in Handling Objections

Step 1. Acknowledge the Prospect's Concern

When you acknowledge objections, you are implying interest in the prospect's concerns and appreciation of the fact that he or she voiced them. If the prospect did not voice objections, you could not resolve them. If you do not resolve them, you will not achieve your sales call objective. When you acknowledge the objection, do not imply that you agree with it. Here are some ways to acknowledge objections:

"That's a good question."

"I appreciate your interest."

"I can understand your concern."

"That's a question I would have, too."

"It's a good idea to consider that point."

"You have every right to question that point."

"I understand how you feel."

Step 2. Clarify the Objection and Identify the Problem/Need

Clarifying an objection means asking questions about it to make sure you fully understand it. What the prospect says and means are often two different things. When the prospect elaborates on the objection, it allows you time to think of what benefits and proof you will use to resolve it. You also regain control of the interview. Clarifying does not mean repeating the objection word for word. Here are some questions that can be used to begin the clarifying process:

"Why do you say that?"

"Would you elaborate on that for me?"

"Please tell me more."

"May I ask why you feel that way?"

Continue asking clarifying questions until the problem or need has been clearly identified. Here is an example:

PROSPECT:	Your price is too high (Price/Money Objection).
SALESPERSON:	That's a good point (Acknowledgment). What price are you paying now (Clarifier)?
PROSPECT:	$37.49 per unit, which is $4 less than your price.
SALESPERSON:	To what model of my competitor's are you referring (Clarifier)?
PROSPECT:	It's their model #2702.
SALESPERSON:	(The problem has been identified.) The #2702 is their discount model. It doesn't have some of the features ours does. Let me show you the difference and why ours is worth $4 more.

Here is another example in which clarifying questions revealed the real objection. The salesperson is selling a $10,000 computer to an office manager.

PROSPECT:	I think I need some more time before I decide (Time Objection).
SALESPERSON:	I can understand how you feel (Acknowledgment). Is there anything in particular you have to think about (Clarifier)?

PROSPECT: No. I just need a little more time.

SALESPERSON: Do you have concerns about this model of computer (Clarifier)?

PROSPECT: No. This is the one our company needs.

SALESPERSON: Is it the $10,000 investment (Clarifier)?

PROSPECT: That's a lot of money. We just can't come up with that much at this time. (Price/Money Objection; problem identified).

The objection started out as a Time Objection, but clarifying questions brought out the real objection; a lack of money. Since the problem has been identified, the salesperson can proceed to Step 3.

Step 3. Provide Features, Benefits, and Proof to Resolve the Objection— Use Dramatization

In the Securing Desire section of the presentation, we used features, advantages, benefits, proof, and dramatization to convince the prospect that our product or service would solve problems or satisfy needs. Remember "FAB+PD?" Your strategy to Handle Objections is the same. Use FAB+PD. Refer to the discussion on pages 59 and 60 concerning these topics.

Your Features-Benefits Worksheet on pages 135 and 136 should provide the information you need to resolve the objections. You may find, however, that it does not have benefits to resolve all your objections. If this is the case, add features, benefits, and proof to the worksheet so all your objections can be resolved.

In the real world, salespeople do not make a sale on every call. Prospects frequently offer objections that cannot be resolved. However, this section is structured to allow salespeople to resolve the objections they get during the Handling Objections role play.

Step 4. Offer a Trial Close

Do not continue with your presentation if the prospect is still voicing an objection. It must be resolved before you can expect to close. A trial close is a question that asks the prospect if you have resolved the objection. If you have, proceed to Step 5. If you have not, go back to Step 2 and start over again. A trial close also gives the prospect another opportunity to give you a buying signal.

These questions are good trial closes:

"Does that answer your question?"

"Have I resolved that issue?"

"Do you have any more questions concerning (objection)?"

"Does that make sense to you?"

"How does that sound?"

"Is this the answer you are seeking?"

"Do you agree this isn't a problem?"

Step 5. Close or Go Back to Step 2 in Securing Desire

If the prospect seems ready to close, do so, even if you have more problems your product or service will solve and benefits to support them. If the prospect does not seem ready to close, go back to Step 2 in Securing Desire. Identify another problem/need and support it with features, benefits, and proof. Refer to the "Steps in a Sales Presentation" diagram on the inside front cover. The arrows illustrate this process.

Example of Handling Objections

The following is an example of the Handling Objections section of the presentation for Fusion.

PLANNING GUIDE—FUSION HANDLING OBJECTIONS

Salesperson-Prospect Dialogue

Need Objection

PROSPECT: *I don't have room on the shelf for another line of running shoes.*

Step 1. Acknowledge concern

SALESPERSON: *I've had other dealers mention that, too.*

Step 2. Clarify

SALESPERSON: *Do you keep a record of sales for each item you stock?*

PROSPECT: *Yes. We have a computerized inventory control system.*

SALESPERSON: *Can we take a look at it?*

PROSPECT: *I'll get it.*

Step 3. Features, benefits, proof, and dramatization

SALESPERSON: *You mentioned earlier that Reebok ERS wasn't selling very well. As you can see here, you have only sold two pairs in the past two months. Penny, you could feature this item at a special price and sell all your stock to make room for Fusion.*

Also, you should consider the fact that this is a specialty store that caters to serious runners. Your customers will be seeing our ads in <u>Runner's World</u>, <u>Running Times</u>, and <u>Michigan Runner</u>. They will be coming to your store with the expectation of being able to buy Fusion.

Plus, Fusion is on the cutting edge of technology. As I mentioned before, we have the Propulsion Plate System and HydroFlow pad. (Give her the samples of the Propulsion Plate and HydroFlow pad again.) These features have been tested and proven to improve performance and reduce injuries. Fusion is superior to the Reebok ERS shoe.

Step 4. Trial close

SALESPERSON: *Wouldn't you agree?*

PLANNING GUIDE—FUSION HANDLING OBJECTIONS *(continued)*

Salesperson-Prospect Dialogue

Product/Service Objection

PROSPECT: *The Nike rep was in the other day and showed me the new 180 Air. I like that shoe better.*

Step 1. Acknowledge concern

SALESPERSON: *The 180 is a good shoe.*

Step 2. Clarify

SALESPERSON: *Penny, what is it that you like about their product?*

PROSPECT: *It has extra cushioning.*

Step 3. Features, benefits, proof, and dramatization

SALESPERSON: *That's true. Nike did make the air bag larger. Also, the term "180" comes from the fact that you can see the air bag 180 degrees around the heel of the shoe. But the shoe does not have any new technology. Nike has had the air bag since 1979 and the fact you can see it doesn't improve a runner's performance.*

Fusion has the Propulsion Plate System and the HydroFlow pad to improve performance and reduce injuries. Recently, Fusion won the "Best Running Shoe" award at the Exhibition of Sports and Leisure in London, England. It was rated superior to the 180 in design, aesthetics, and value. (Show article, which details the ratings.) The expert judges felt that Fusion is a superior shoe.

Step 4. Trial close

SALESPERSON: *Have I resolved that issue?*

PLANNING GUIDE—FUSION HANDLING OBJECTIONS *(continued)*

Salesperson-Prospect Dialogue

Source Objection

PROSPECT: *Brooks is a small company compared to Nike and Reebok.*

Step 1. Acknowledge concern

SALESPERSON: *Size is something to consider.*

Step 2. Clarify

SALESPERSON: *Could you be more specific, Penny?*

PROSPECT: *They probably spend a lot more money in research and development than Brooks does.*

Step 3. Features, benefits, proof, and dramatization

SALESPERSON: *You may be right. I don't know how much they spend in R & D. I do know, however, that since 1975, Brooks has led the way in new running shoe technology. (Show "Technical Highlights" page.)*

Here is a chronological list of some of our innovations. In 1975, Brooks was the first to introduce the ethylene vinyl acetate (EVA) midsole for improved cushioning. The Diagonal Rollbar was introduced in 1982. It reduces excessive side-to-side motion, which reduces injuries. In 1986, it was the Kinetic Wedge. This feature allows the foot to move in a natural motion, which reduces fatigue. HydroFlow came along in 1989. And now it's the Propulsion Plate System.

These innovations were developed by an expert team of worldclass runners, scientists, and engineers, along with the Biomechanics Evaluation Lab at Michigan State University. So you can be assured that when you buy a Brooks shoe, you are getting the best that technology has to offer.

Step 4. Trial close

SALESPERSON: *Does that answer your question?*

PLANNING GUIDE—FUSION HANDLING OBJECTIONS *(continued)*

Salesperson-Prospect Dialogue

Price-Money Objection

PROSPECT: *What is your price?*

SALESPERSON: *Our suggested retail price is $124.95.*

PROSPECT: *My customers won't pay that much for a shoe.*

Step 1. Acknowledge concern

SALESPERSON: *I'm glad you raised that issue, Penny.*

Step 2. Clarify

SALESPERSON: *Do you stock any shoes that are priced over $100?*

PROSPECT: *The Nike Air Max is priced at $110.*

SALESPERSON: *What kind of turnover does it have?*

PROSPECT: *Pretty good but not the best.*

Step 3. Features, benefits, proof, and dramatization

SALESPERSON: *It's incredible what people will pay for state-of-the-art athletic products these days. A good tennis racquet costs over $250, and it's hard to find a nice set of golf clubs for under $500. As I mentioned before, Penny, Fusion is designed for the serious runners who shop in your store. They want the latest technology and will pay for it, provided it is a good value.*

I have a list here that shows how good a value Fusion is. (Show "Value" visual aid.) First, I have mentioned that Fusion will dramatically improve running performance due to the Propulsion Plate System. Second, the HydroFlow pad provides cushioning, which will reduce foot, ankle, and knee injuries. Third, we have an anatomically correct fit, which improves comfort, and an extremely durable outsole so it lasts longer. And finally, Fusion offers contemporary styling. These features make Fusion an outstanding value, which will result in high sales and profits for this store.

Step 4. Trial close

SALESPERSON: *Considering these factors, would you agree Fusion is a good value?*

PLANNING GUIDE—FUSION HANDLING OBJECTIONS *(continued)*

Salesperson-Prospect Dialogue

Time Objection

PROSPECT: *It's only February. Why don't you come back after the weather breaks?*

Step 1. Acknowledge concern

SALESPERSON: *I understand how you feel.*

Step 2. Clarify

SALESPERSON: *When do sales of your running shoes begin to pick up?*

PROSPECT: *Around the first of April.*

Step 3. Features, benefits, proof, and dramatization

SALESPERSON: *That's when most of my dealers experience a big surge in sales. I mentioned earlier that our advertising for Fusion begins with the April issues of* Runner's World, Running Times, *and* Michigan Runner. *These publications hit the newsstands on March 15th. If you wait until April to place your order, you will miss out on the sales our initial ads will generate. And you will have a lot of disappointed customers.*

Step 4. Trial close

SALESPERSON: *You don't want to disappoint your customers and pass up those sales and profits, do you Penny?*

Preparing to Role Play

Planning Guide Form—Handling Objections

The Planning Guide that follows will help you apply what you have learned about handling objections. Identify one objection for each of the Five Buying Decisions. *Make sure they are not questions.* Questions merely ask for more information. Then turn to your Features-Benefits Worksheet on pages 135 and 136. Use the features, benefits, proof, and dramatization to resolve each objection in the Planning Guide. If you find you lack some benefits, add them to the worksheet. Finally, add acknowledgment, clarifying, and trial close statements to the Planning Guide. Be sure to provide a complete dialogue of what you and the prospect say. Complete the forms neatly in number 2 pencil so they can be changed and photocopied. Study the Rating Form on page 95 to make sure you have not forgotten anything.

PLANNING GUIDE—HANDLING OBJECTIONS

Salesperson-Prospect Dialogue

Refer to the example of the completed Planning Guide on pages 83 through 87.

Need Objection *(Write the prospect's objection here as a declarative statement not a question. Fill this form out neatly in number 2 pencil.)*

Step 1. Acknowledge concern *(See page 80.)*

Step 2. Clarify *(See pages 80 and 81.)*

Step 3. Features, benefits, proof, and dramatization *(Refer to your Features-Benefits Worksheet on pages 135 and 136. Also, see page 76.)*

Step 4. Trial close *(See page 81.)*

PLANNING GUIDE—HANDLING OBJECTIONS *(continued)*

Salesperson-Prospect Dialogue

Product/Service Objection *(Write the prospect's objection here.)*

Step 1. Acknowledge concern *(Use a different acknowledgment statement than the first one.)*

Step 2. Clarify *(Use a different clarifying question than the first one.)*

Step 3. Features, benefits, proof, and dramatization

Step 4. Trial close *(Use a different trial close than the first one.)*

PLANNING GUIDE—HANDLING OBJECTIONS *(continued)*

Salesperson-Prospect Dialogue

Source Objection *(This is an objection related to doing business with you or your company.)*

Step 1. Acknowledge concern

Step 2. Clarify

Step 3. Features, benefits, proof, and dramatization

Step 4. Trial close

PLANNING GUIDE—HANDLING OBJECTIONS *(continued)*

Salesperson-Prospect Dialogue

Price-Money Objection *(PROSPECT: Be sure you know what the price is before you offer this objection.)*

Step 1. Acknowledge concern

Step 2. Clarify

Step 3. Features, benefits, proof, and dramatization *(Refer to pages 76 and 77 for ideas to resolve price objections.)*

Step 4. Trial close

PLANNING GUIDE—HANDLING OBJECTIONS *(continued)*

Salesperson-Prospect Dialogue

Time Objection *(This is an objection related to allowing you to achieve your call objective during this sales call.)*

Step 1. Acknowledge concern

Step 2. Clarify

Step 3. Features, benefits, proof, and dramatization *(Use one of the "Buy Now Methods" of closing the sale on page 99 to resolve this objection.)*

Step 4. Trial close

How the Role Play Will Be Conducted

Your sales manager may have you role play Handling Objections. If not, you should role play it on your own or with two other people. Look over the instructions on page 43. You will not be role playing the Approach or Securing Desire, only Handling Objections. Begin seated at the prospect's desk.

The prospect will allow you to resolve each objection with one counterbenefit. (In the real world, it may take several counters to resolve an objection, and some objections you may not be able to resolve at all.) You should respond to each using the four steps you have learned. Do not try to close the sale. Stop at the last trial close.

Materials Needed to Role Play Handling Objections

You will need your Setting the Scene form on page 39, five-page Planning Guide, a photocopy of the Planning Guide for the prospect, Handling Objections rating form, product samples, visual aids, and *RPPS* manual. If you do not have access to a photocopy machine to reproduce your Planning Guide for the prospect, make a typewritten or handwritten copy of the salesperson-prospect dialogue, excluding Steps 3 and 4 for each objection. Include the titles of the steps.

Handling Objections Rating Form (25 Points)

Salesperson's Company: _____   Hour: _____

Product/Service: _____   Salesperson's Name: _____

Prospect's Company: _____	Possible Score	Actual Score		
		Record Scores of Three Role Plays		
—Ability to acknowledge the prospect's concern after each objection	2	_____	_____	_____
—Ability to clarify each objection	4	_____	_____	_____
—Ability to provide features and benefits relevant to each objection	7	_____	_____	_____
—Ability to offer proof, when appropriate	4	_____	_____	_____
—Ability to use visual (and/or audio) aids where appropriate	3	_____	_____	_____
—Ability to offer a trial close after each objection	2	_____	_____	_____
—Ability to be enthusiastic, smile, and use the prospect's name	3	_____	_____	_____
Total	25 pts.	_____	_____	_____

Coach's notes and comments:

CLOSING THE SALE AND BUILDING CUSTOMER RELATIONS

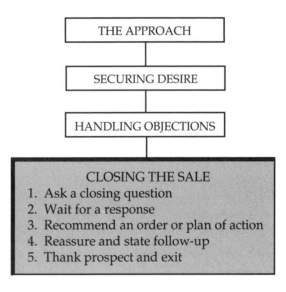

Objective of the Close

The ultimate goal of any sales presentation is Closing the Sale. At this point in the presentation you get a commitment from the prospect for an order or a plan of action. Closing is achieving your sales call objective.

Preparing to Close the Sale

When to Close

Inexperienced salespeople often wonder when it is appropriate to try to Close the Sale. You should close when the prospect indicates he or she is ready to close. This can be at the beginning, middle, or end of the presentation. Often it is after you have asked a trial close question. Whenever the prospect gives you a buying signal, try to close the sale.

A buying signal is anything a person does or says that suggests he or she is ready to buy. You must listen to and observe the prospect to identify signals. The following is a list of common buying signals.

1. After successfully handling a major objection

   Salesperson: "Have I resolved the issue of price for you?"
       Prospect: "I can see it's worth the price."

2. When the prospect gives enthusiastic agreement to a benefit

   "Our company could really use something like that."
   "That's exactly what we've been looking for."
   "That *would* solve a problem we've been having."

3. When the prospect asks questions that suggest he or she is ready to buy

   "When can you deliver?"
   "What sizes does it come in?"
   "Do you offer any discounts?"
   "Is that item in stock?"
   "Do you charge for installation?"

4. When the prospect provides nonverbal signs that suggest he or she is ready to buy

   Suddenly relaxes body.
   Nods head in approval.
   Smiles in agreement.
   Picks up the product and examines it closely.
   Begins to read the sales agreement.

5. At the end of the presentation

You may get several buying signals throughout the presentation. Each time you do, try to close. If the prospect is not ready to be closed, he or she will ask for more information or offer an objection. Provide the information or resolve the objection, then try to close again if you get a buying signal.

Closing Methods

There are a number of different methods to Close the Sale. It is important to know how to use several, because no single method is appropriate under all circumstances. Below are five of the most common ones.

Direct Method—Ask for a commitment directly.

   "Do I have your commitment to buy this word processor?"

   "May we schedule a tour of our hotel and meeting rooms?"

   "Can I count on you to begin using our agency to book all of your executive travel beginning the first of the month?"

Minor Point Method—Rather than asking the prospect *if* he or she wants to buy, ask *what, when,* or *how* he or she wants to buy.

   "How about installation next week?"

   "Would delivery the first of the month be soon enough?"

   "Should this purchase be billed to the home office?"

   "Should the order be marked RUSH?"

Alternative Choice Method—Ask the prospect which of two variations is desired. The choices could be between such things as two models, colors, delivery dates, installation dates, payment plans, or quantities to buy.

   "May we begin offering our service this week or is next week best for you?"

   "Would this model or our deluxe model best suit your needs?"

"Shall we write the order for 1,000 units or would 750 be enough?"

"Would you rather lease or buy the equipment?"

Buy Now Method—Provide some reason why the prospect should buy today rather than waiting, then ask for a commitment.

Trial offer: "I can see that you have some reservations to buying our FAX machine today. Why don't I bring one over and let you try it out for a week free of charge. Okay?"

Standing Room Only: "Our hotel meeting rooms get booked up really fast. If you don't reserve the rooms for your meeting today, they may not be available. Do I have your commitment?"

Impending event: "Our price is going up $215 in four weeks. If you buy now, I can guarantee you this price. Shall we write up the order?"

Concession: "Normally we don't do this, but if you'll buy now, I'll give you a one-year service contract at half price. Okay?"

Ideal time to buy: "As soon as the weather breaks, a lot more people will be playing tennis. If you buy now, the tennis rackets will be in your store and you can begin to realize all the profits we talked about. What do you say?"

Summary Method—Briefly summarize three or four major benefits you mentioned in the presentation, then ask for a commitment. Your last benefit should be the general benefit you mentioned in the Approach.

"Let me summarize the major benefits we've talked about this morning, Mr. Jones. First, our sales training workshop is a comprehensive program that will improve the skills of both your new and experienced salespeople. Second, they will learn how to conduct better sales presentations and manage their time more productively. And finally, your company will experience an increase in sales and profits. Shall we go ahead with it?"

Notice that all five closing methods end with a question. You must ask for a commitment to Close the Sale.

Attitude Toward Closing

To be successful in Closing the Sale you must have the proper closing attitude. First, expect that you will close during your sales call. If you do not possess this positive attitude, and this confidence in your company and product or service, the prospect will sense it and be less likely to buy. Second, provide only the features, benefits, proof, and visual aids necessary to close. Your mission is not to overwhelm the prospect with your knowledge of your industry, company, and product or service. Finally, do not be afraid to ask for a commitment. The prospect will respond to your closing question by either agreeing to buy, offering an objection, or asking for more problems or needs to be addressed with features and benefits. Regardless of the response, you will know what to do. If the prospect's response is favorable, continue the closing sequence. If an objection is offered, handle it using the steps discussed in Chapter 7, then try to close again if you get a buying signal. If the prospect feels he or she must be shown how the product or service can solve more problems or satisfy more needs, return to Securing Desire. Remember prospects expect to be asked for the order. They want you to help them make the decision to buy. So ask a closing question and Close the Sale.

Building Customer Relations through Follow-up

Most of this text has focused on developing and conducting an effective sales presentation for a prospect. In the short term, good presentations will have a substantial impact on sales. However, in the long term, establishing positive relationships with customers by following up after the initial presentation will result in even greater sales. Assume, for example, that you are a salesperson for Brooks Shoe, Inc., calling on a sporting goods buyer. The initial order for the Fusion running shoe might be $1,500. If you go out of your way to make sure the buyer is happy with the initial purchase, it will increase the buyer's confidence in you and your company. Provided the product generates sufficient turnover, the loyalty and goodwill created could result in future sales of tens of thousands of dollars. Follow-up activities, such as those listed next, will enable you to build customer relations and long-term sales volume.

After the initial presentation, contact the customer in person, by letter, or by telephone to:

1. Ensure satisfaction after delivery of your product or use of your service. Make sure the customer's needs were satisfied.
2. Report the status of open orders, including production schedules, the availability of products or services, or delivery dates to keep the customer informed of progress.
3. Initiate installation, maintenance, or repairs of the product.
4. Schedule engineers or technicians to meet with the customer.
5. Train customer personnel on how to operate the product (e.g., a photocopy machine).
6. Train wholesale or retail customer salespeople how to sell the product.
7. Send or deliver additional brochures, literature, proposals, or contracts.
8. Help build a display or merchandise the product in retail stores.
9. Answer customer questions related to the purchase.
10. Handle customer complaints, such as late delivery, product quality problems, out-of-stock conditions, billing errors, or damaged goods during shipment.
11. Schedule a meeting to make another sales presentation. Discover new needs and get additional orders.
12. Get referrals for new prospects.

Some salespeople go beyond the activities mentioned here and send "thank you" letters to customers when they buy, birthday and Christmas cards, and personal notes of congratulations when buyers earn promotions. In summary, consider that most successful salespeople have a *long-term* perspective on solving customer problems and satisfying their needs. Be sure to build relationships through extensive follow-up activities and providing good customer service.

Steps in Closing the Sale

Step 1. Ask a Closing Question

When you get a buying signal, often after a trial close, ask for a commitment using an appropriate closing method. The Direct Method can be used any time. The Minor Point Method is excellent when the prospect seems afraid to make a decision. If the prospect seems interested and has narrowed his or her choices somewhat, try the Alternative Choice Method. The Buy Now Method is appropriate when you get a time objection. At the end of the presentation, the Summary Method is a good choice. Since you may have several opportunities to Close the Sale, use the method that is appropriate for the existing circumstances.

Step 2. Wait For a Response

When you have asked a closing question, there may be a period of silence. Don't be afraid of the silence. The prospect is considering the Five Buying Decisions: "Do I *need* this type of product?" "Will this brand of *product* satisfy my needs?" "Is this the *source* from whom I should buy?" "Is the *price* right?" and "Is the *time* to buy now?" Let the prospect be the first one to speak after you have asked a closing question. If you talk first, you may lose this chance to close. If the prospect is not ready to be closed, he or she will either ask for more information or offer an objection. If so, provide the information or handle the objection, then try to close again if you get a buying signal.

Step 3. Recommend an Order or Plan of Action and Confirm the Details

If your sales call objective is to write an order or get a contract signed, have one to fill out during your presentation. If you do not have an order form, make one up like the one for Fusion on page 102. Recommend a specific quantity, considering what is realistic for the prospect to buy. Confirm the delivery date and billing and shipping addresses. If the prospect is going to resell the product, be sure to stress the profit per unit and total profits for the quantity you are recommending. The profit benefit helps justify the investment being made. Here is how the dialogue might sound if you were selling Fusion to a sporting goods buyer:

SALESPERSON: Shall we write up the order for 18 pairs of the men's sizes (Direct Close)?

PROSPECT: Yes, I guess so.

SALESPERSON: (Pulls out the order form and begins filling it out. The sample order form is on page 102.) Okay, that's 18 pairs of our item number 4870, Fusion shoes.

The unit price is $67 per pair. That comes to a total investment of $1,206. Now since you'll have a 46 percent markup on this item, you'll enjoy profits of $57.95 per pair and total profits of $1,043.10 for this order.

When do you want delivery?

PROSPECT: The first of the month would be soon enough.

SALESPERSON: (Writes the date on the order form.) Is this the correct address for shipping and billing?

PROSPECT: Yes it is.

SALESPERSON: If you would just authorize the paperwork, we can start processing the order right away. (Salesperson gives the order form and a pen to the prospect.)

Your sales call objective might be such that it is not appropriate to write an order. For example, if you were selling the use of meeting rooms for a hotel to a sales manager, your sales call objective might be to convince him or her to accompany you to the hotel to see your facilities. Rather than writing an order, you are requesting a plan of action. You would be combining Steps 1, 2, and 3. Here's how the dialogue might go:

SALESPERSON: Let me make a suggestion. Why don't we set up a time that would be convenient for you to come down to our hotel and see our facilities (plan of action)? Would this week or next week be best for you (Alternative Choice Method)?

PROSPECT: (Looks at calendar.) This week is bad. Next Tuesday looks good.

SALESPERSON: That's perfect. How about 11:30? That way we can have lunch so you can see how good our food is.

PROSPECT: Fine.

SALESPERSON: Why don't I pick you up here at 11:30 next Tuesday (confirm the details)?

PROSPECT: Okay.

ORDER FORM

BROOKS SHOE, INC.
9341 Courtland Dr.
Rockford, MI 49351
616-866-5500

BILL TO: Taylor Sports, Inc.
2122 Main Street
Grand Rapids, MI
49507

DATE OF ORDER: February 4, 19—
SHIP ON: March 1, 19—
SALESPERSON: J. Dykehouse

Quantity	Item Number	Description	Unit Price	Total Amount
18 pairs	4870	Fusion Shoes – Men's Sizes 7, 7½, 8, 11½, 12, 13 one pair of each. Balance of sizes two pairs each.	$67.00 per pair	$1,206.00
		Total Amount of Order		$1,206.00

SHIP TO:

Same as above.

Penny Taylor
Buyer's Name—Print

Penny Taylor
Buyer's Signature

Step 4. Reassure the Prospect and State Your Follow-up Plan

People often have misgivings about something they buy. They wonder if they have made the right decision. They feel better about the decision if they are reassured. Give the prospects a verbal pat on the back. Tell them that they have made the right decision to accept your proposal.

Prospects also want to know that you are going to make sure the order or plan of action they have agreed to will be taken care of properly. By stating your follow-up plan, you are confirming to them that you appreciate their trust and

FUSION

For the athlete who understands the physical benefits of performance engineered equipment and demands state-of-the-art technology. For the athlete "...who wants a 'do everything' shoe..."[1]

Construction
- Slip-lasted

Outsole
- Clear silicone rubber
- State-of-the-art high abrasion rubber webwork design

Midsole
- Tri-density compression molded EVA
- Propulsion Plate™ system with full length carbon fiber contour plate offers exceptional stability, cushioning and performance for efficiency of push off during the forward phase of running
- Rearfoot HydroFlow™ custom cushioning
- Modified diagonal rollbar
- Forefoot visco-elastic pad
- TPR heel counter
- Combination of midsole componentry produces a system that doesn't break down or bottom out

Upper
- Ventilated nylon mesh and teijin
- Reflective trim
- Speed lacing system
- HydroTech sockliner for moisture-wicking and cushioning

4870 Men's • Purple/Orange/White • Sizes 5-12,13
3598 Women's • Purple/Orange/White • Sizes 6-10,11

The Fusion is a training shoe which incorporates a full length contour Propulsion Plate offering exceptional stability, cushioning, and performance.

The contour propulsion plate is designed to achieve a specific spring quality for the activity of running. Carbon fiber is an elastic material possessing great strength and durability, but is extremely lightweight.

The contour propulsion plate incorporates a rearfoot stability component, an external arch support, and a forefoot propulsion component. The external arch provides exceptional stability while at the same time storing energy during foot pronation. The propulsion component of the plate design assists the foot in providing more efficient push off.

[1]Reprinted with permission from America's Athletics Magazine, Fall/Winter 1990, "The Six Best New Shoes!" by Gary Doettelmann. For subscription information: 1 year $17.95, P.O. Box 1499, Los Altos, CA 94040.

will not consider your job complete until they reap the benefits of the purchase. Refer to the follow-up activities discussed on page 100. Use one that is appropriate for your product or service. This portion of Closing the Sale for Fusion might sound like this:

SALESPERSON: You have definitely made the right decision to buy Fusion, Penny. It is going to be the big winner in the running shoe category this season (reassure).

        What I'll do is input your order tonight and make a point to come back just after you receive your shipment, so I can put up some of our point-of-sale material. I'll also have brochures that will explain the benefits of Fusion to your salespeople and customers (follow-up).

The sales representative for the hotel might say:

SALESPERSON: Your time will be well spent when you come down and see our facility. It's perfect for your needs (reassure).

        When I get back to the office I'll check and make sure the date you want is open. Would it be all right if I call you this afternoon to confirm it (follow-up)?

Begin to pack up your samples and visual aids in preparation for your exit.

Step 5. Thank the Prospect and Exit

Since the prospect has just agreed to do what you want, you should show your appreciation by thanking him or her. Do not spend time bringing up more benefits or idle small talk. It might give the prospect time to come up with an objection you cannot resolve. You have achieved your sales call objective, so pack up your visual aids and exit. Be sure to smile and shake hands on the way out.

Example of Closing the Sale

Following is an example of the Closing the Sale section of the presentation for Fusion. Note that there are closing questions for each of the five methods discussed in this chapter. Steps 3, 4, and 5 would be the same regardless of the closing method used.

PLANNING GUIDE—FUSION CLOSING THE SALE

Salesperson-Prospect Dialogue

Step 1. Ask a closing question

DIRECT METHOD

SALESPERSON: *Shall we write up an order for Fusion?*

MINOR POINT METHOD

SALESPERSON: *Would delivery on March 1st be soon enough?*

ALTERNATIVE CHOICE METHOD

SALESPERSON: *Our women's line will be out in mid-April, Penny. Do you want to order the men's and women's line today, or do you want to wait until next month to place your order for the women's line?*

PROSPECT: *Let's go ahead with just the men's line for now.*

BUY NOW METHOD

SALESPERSON: *(Standing Room Only) The demand for this shoe is going to be very high this spring. If you place your order today, Penny, I can guarantee we will have adequate inventory to meet your needs. Do I have your commitment?*

SUMMARY METHOD

SALESPERSON: *Let me summarize the major benefits we've talked about this morning, Penny. First, the HydroFlow pad and Propulsion Plate System will improve running performance and reduce injuries. Second, our advertising and promotional program will create awareness for Fusion resulting in high sales in your store. And finally, Fusion will increase the profits of your athletic shoe department. Shall we go ahead with it?*

PLANNING GUIDE—FUSION CLOSING THE SALE *(continued)*

Salesperson-Prospect Dialogue

Step 2. Wait for a response

Step 3. Recommend an order and confirm the details

SALESPERSON: *(Get order form and fill it out.) I recommend that your initial order be 18 pairs; one pair for sizes 7, 7½, 8, 11½, 12, and 13. We should double up on the more popular sizes. Okay?*

PROSPECT: *What's my total cost?*

SALESPERSON: *Let's see. The investment is $67 per pair times 18 pairs. $1,206. And the profit per unit at our suggested retail price of $124.95 is $57.95. So your total profits for this order are $1,043.10. Not bad! Wouldn't you agree?*

PROSPECT: *Let's go ahead with it.*

SALESPERSON: *Would delivery the first of the month be soon enough?*

PROSPECT: *Yes.*

SALESPERSON: *Is this the correct address for shipping and billing?*

PROSPECT: *Yes it is.*

SALESPERSON: *If you would just authorize the paperwork, we can start processing the order right away. (Give order form and pen to the prospect.)*

Step 4. Reassure the prospect and state your follow-up plan

SALESPERSON: *You have definitely made the right decision to buy Fusion, Penny. It is going to be the big winner in the running shoe category this season.*

What I'll do is input your order tonight and make a point to come back just after you receive your shipment, so I can put up some of our point-of-sale material. I'll also have some information that will explain the benefits of Fusion to your salespeople.

Step 5. Thank the prospect and exit.

SALESPERSON: *Thanks very much, Penny. I'll see you in about four weeks.*

Preparing to Role Play

Planning Guide Form—Closing the Sale

You can now apply the principles you have learned about Closing the Sale to your own product or service. For each closing method in the following Planning Guide, write down the exact wording of your closing question. Note the wording for the other steps, too. If you plan to write an order on your call, make up an order form like the one on page 102, unless you were able to secure one from your company. Complete the Planning Guide forms neatly in number 2 pencil so they can be changed and photocopied. Look over the rating form on page 111 to make sure you have not forgotten anything.

PLANNING GUIDE—FUSION CLOSING THE SALE

Salesperson-Prospect Dialogue

Refer to the example of the completed Planning Guide on pages 105 and 106.

PROSPECT: If you are purchasing something, be sure you know what the price is before you allow the salesperson to close the sale.

Step 1. Ask a closing question. *(Fill out this form neatly in number 2 pencil. Write small.)*

DIRECT METHOD *(Write your closing question here. See pages 98 and 99.)*

MINOR POINT METHOD

ALTERNATIVE CHOICE METHOD

BUY NOW METHOD

SUMMARY METHOD

PLANNING GUIDE—CLOSING THE SALE *(continued)*

Salesperson-Prospect Dialogue

Step 2. Wait for response

Step 3. Recommend an order or plan of action and confirm the details *(Steps 3, 4, and 5 are the same regardless of the closing method you used on the previous page. See pages 101 and 102.)*

Step 4. Reassure the prospect and state your follow-up plan *(See pages 102 and 104.)*

Step 5. Thank the prospect and exit *(See page 104.)*

How the Role Play Will Be Conducted

Your sales manager may have you role play Closing the Sale. If not, do so on your own to ensure you are prepared for the final presentation. Review the instructions in the section "How the Role Play Will be Conducted" on page 43. You will role play only the close, so you will begin seated at the prospect's desk. The prospect should not give the salesperson any objections, but should allow the salesperson to close the sale each time he or she is asked a closing question.

You will role play three closes using three of the five closing methods. One is not contingent on the other. Go through Step 3 (recommend an order or plan of action), Step 4 (reassure the prospect), and Step 5 (thank the prospect and exit) *only on the first closing method* you are using. After you have role played a complete close, sit down again and role play two more closing methods. Here's what the salesperson, prospect, and coach should do:

1. Coach assigns three closing methods to the salesperson.
2. Salesperson gives the prospect the photocopy of the Planning Guides and "sets the scene."
3. Salesperson states which closing method will be used first.
4. Salesperson asks a closing question using the closing method and does a complete close, including recommending an order or a plan of action, reassuring and stating his or her follow-up, and thanking the prospect and exiting. The coach fills out the rating form. This closing sequence is completed.
5. Salesperson sits down and states what closing method will be used next. The salesperson asks a closing question using the closing method but does not go through Steps 3, 4, or 5, only Steps 1 and 2.
6. Repeat point 5 for the third closing method. The role play is now completed.

Materials Needed to Role Play Closing the Sale

You will need your Setting the Scene form on page 39, two-page completed Planning Guide, a photocopy of the Planning Guide for the prospect, the Closing the Sale rating form, and *RPPS* manual. If you are writing an order during the close, have an order form to complete in the presence of the prospect. Also bring a pen so the prospect can sign it. The prospect can ad lib all responses during the close, so if you do not have access to a photocopy machine to reproduce your Planning Guide for your prospect, the role play can be conducted without it.

Closing the Sale Rating Form (25 Points)

Salesperson's Company: _____   Hour: _____

Product/Service: _____   Salesperson's Name: _____

Prospect's Company: _____

	Possible Score	Actual Score
		Record Scores of Three Role Plays
—Ability to use Closing Method 1 properly	4	_____ _____ _____
—Ability to wait for a response, recommend an order or plan of action, and confirm the details. (If an order was required, did the salesperson have an order form? If the product is going to be resold, were profits per unit and total profits mentioned?)	4	_____ _____ _____
—Ability to reassure the prospect and state a follow-up plan	4	_____ _____ _____
—Ability to thank the prospect and exit properly	2	_____ _____ _____
—Ability to use Closing Method 2 properly	4	_____ _____ _____
—Ability to use Closing Method 3 properly	4	_____ _____ _____
—Ability to be enthusiastic, smile, and use the prospect's name	3	_____ _____ _____
Total	25 pts.	_____ _____ _____

Coach's notes and comments:

ROLE PLAYING THE COMPLETE SALES PRESENTATION

Other Characteristics of an Effective Sales Presentation

While this text has provided most of what you need to know to conduct an effective presentation, the following are some additional suggestions.

1. Focus your attention on the prospect, not on your product or service.
2. Establish a dialogue (two-way communication), not a monologue, to maintain the prospect's interest and attention.
3. Maintain control, but do not show it. Prospects can be intimidated by high-pressure salespeople. Ask questions, offer choices, and request assistance.
4. Put visual aids directly in front of the prospect.
5. If you do a demonstration, get the prospect physically involved in it.
6. Use proper body language. Maintain eye contact and smile.
7. Avoid objectionable mannerisms, such as chewing gum, tapping your feet, and repeating yourself with "and-ah," "umh," etc.
8. Use the proper speed of delivery, not too fast or too slow.
9. Keep your presentation brief and to the point. Do not be wordy.
10. Maintain a positive, enthusiastic attitude.
11. Project poise and confidence.
12. Adapt your presentation to the personality style of the prospect.

Personality Styles of Prospects

Every prospect has a different personality. A salesperson must adapt his or her selling style and presentation to the prospect's personality if the sales presentation is to be successful. This adaptation can be particularly difficult on the first meeting with a prospect. The way the prospect responded on the telephone when you called to set up an appointment may give you a clue as to his or her personality, but you cannot be sure until you meet face-to-face. The following are suggestions on how to adapt your presentation, given the personality of the prospect.

Social Personality—Warm, friendly, and indecisive. Has a tendency to talk incessantly and get off the subject. Use an aggressive, hard-sell approach and appeal to emotions. If the prospect spends too much time on idle chit chat, use questions to direct the conversation back to the presentation.

Analytical Personality—Shy, logical, and objective. Asks a lot of questions about the technical details of the product or service. Use facts, figures, and other information (e.g., durability, quality, and dependability) to appeal to the prospect's rational nature. A low-pressure selling style will be the most effective.

Dominant Personality—Cold, aggressive, and opinionated. Tries to rush the salesperson and may attempt to take control of the presentation. Use a concise presentation. Make your points and move on. If he or she is in a hurry during the Approach, you may have to delete Step 2 ("establish a rapport") and go directly to your general benefit. Try to maintain control of the presentation without showing it by asking questions and keeping him or her involved.

Preparing to Role Play the Complete Presentation

Now that you are familiar with the four major sections of a sales presentation, you are ready to put them together and role play a complete sales presentation. You will be expected to apply everything you have learned in this text. If you have role played each of the four sections of the presentation, you are already well prepared to role play the complete presentation. If you have not, begin your preparation by reviewing each of the four parts of a presentation and role play them.

A successful preparation process involves the following steps:

1. Read the section you are going to role play in this text, especially the example provided for selling Fusion.
2. Review your Planning Guide for this part of the presentation.
3. Role play *out loud* by yourself. You must get used to hearing yourself say the words.
4. Evaluate yourself using the appropriate rating form.
5. Repeat 3 and 4 until you feel comfortable with it.
6. Role play with someone acting as a prospect.
7. Evaluate yourself using the appropriate rating form.
8. Repeat 6 and 7 until you are doing everything properly.
9. Role play the complete presentation several times with someone. Tape it and evaluate yourself using the Final Sales Presentation Rating Form on pages 117 and 118.

This process will take at least ten hours over a three- or four-day period to be properly prepared. On the day you are scheduled to give your presentation, get up early, shower, eat a good breakfast, and spend one hour listening to the tape of your role plays and two hours rehearsing your presentation *out loud*. Evaluate yourself after each role play using the Final Sales Presentation Rating Form.

Anyone involved in role playing or making an actual sales call gets nervous— even experienced sales representatives. Reread the section on "Overcoming Fear" on page 2.

How the Role Play Will Be Conducted

Your professor may assign another student to be your prospect. If so, he or she will give the *original copies* of your Planning Guide forms to the student a couple of days before you are scheduled to role play. You must keep a photocopy of these forms. If the nature of your product or service specifically requires a male or a female prospect, let your professor know ahead of time.

Your professor may require that you dress in the type of attire a sales representative selling your product or service would wear. In most cases, this means a suit or sport coat and tie for men and a skirt, dress, or suit for women. Sales representatives in some industries do not wear formal dress. For example, someone selling roofing and siding, burglar alarm systems, or vacuum cleaners to homeowners might wear sport clothes. Find out what a sales representative with your company wears and dress accordingly.

When you are Securing Desire, you should identify one, two, or three problems/needs and support them with appropriate benefits and features. You should attempt to Close the Sale each time you are given a buying signal, even if you have not completed offering all your benefits and features. You will not lose points for closing early, but you will lose points if you fail to attempt to close when you are given a buying signal.

Your prospect will lose points if he or she allows you to close before you have been given at least three objections. If the prospect allows you to close early, do so. If your professor feels you have not had an opportunity to demonstrate your ability to Secure Desire or Handle Objections, he or she will allow you to role play the portions that you did not do the first time. You will not have to repeat anything, just role play what was left out.

The prospect may present you with a time objection that involves getting approval from another decision maker. Acknowledge and clarify the objection and try to convince him or her to give you a commitment without the other person's approval. Use the Buy Now Method to resolve the objection.

The guidelines in the section "How the Role Play Will Be Conducted" on page 43 are still in effect. Since your prospect will already have your Planning Guide forms, you will not have to provide them when you role play. You cannot call "time out," use your Planning Guides, or use any notes other than visual aids when you role play your complete presentation. Be sure to set the scene before the role play begins.

Guidelines for Being a Prospect

You will be evaluated by the coach(es) if you are a prospect, so thorough preparation is necessary. Study the Planning Guide forms you have been given. You will be required to offer at least three objections. A time objection might be appropriate at the end of the presentation. Do not offer objections as questions, but as statements. Ask appropriate questions, take an active part in the presentation, and make sure you sound conversational. Your professor will inform you if you have to dress in any particular attire and if you can have the Planning Guide forms with you to refer to during the role play.

Guidelines for Being an Observer

If you are assigned the task of evaluating a presentation, use the Final Sales Presentation Rating Form in this text. If you will be evaluating a number of presentations, your professor will give you several copies of the rating form. Fill out each section as it is completed rather than waiting until the end of the presentation. Space is provided between the skills for your comments. Evaluate the prospect as well as the salesperson.

Materials Needed to Role Play the Complete Presentation

Review the sections on the materials needed for the Approach (page 43), Securing Desire (page 71), Handling Objections (page 94), and Closing the Sale (page 110).

Final Sales Presentation Rating Form (100 Points)

Salesperson's Company: _____   Hour: _____

Product/Service: _____   Salesperson's Name: _____

Prospect's Company: _____

	Possible Score	Actual Score
Approach Skills		
—Ability to wear appropriate dress	5	_____
—Ability to introduce yourself and company, shake the prospect's hand, offer a business card, and be seated	5	_____
—Ability to establish a rapport, state your purpose, and offer a general benefit	5	_____
—Ability to explain your reason for needing information and offer fact-finding questions to determine the prospect's current situation	5	_____
Securing Desire Skills		
—Ability to briefly familiarize the prospect with your company	5	_____
—Ability to ask questions to identify problems/needs and confirm the prospect's desire to solve each one	5	_____
—Ability to provide features and benefits relevant to each problem/need and offer proof where appropriate	10	_____
—Ability to use visual or audio aids where appropriate and offer a trial close after each benefit statement	5	_____
Handling Objections Skills		
—Ability to acknowledge the prospect's concern and clarify each objection	5	_____
—Ability to provide features and benefits relevant to each objection and offer proof when appropriate	10	_____
—Ability to use visual or audio aids where appropriate and offer a trial close after each objection	5	_____

Closing Skills

—Ability to recognize buying signals and know when to ask a closing   5   _____
question at each appropriate opportunity

—Ability to wait for a response, recommend an order or plan of action,   5   _____
and confirm the details

—Ability to reassure the prospect, state a follow-up plan, thank the   5   _____
prospect, and exit properly

Other Skills

—Ability to maintain the prospect's interest and attention throughout the   5   _____
presentation and to get the prospect involved

—Ability to use the prospect's name, power words, and picture words   5   _____

—Ability to project enthusiasm, poise, and confidence   5   _____

—Ability to maintain good eye contact, smile, and avoid objectionable   5   _____
mannerisms

                                                    Total   100 pts.   _____

Prospect's Skills

Prospect's Name: _____

—Ability to ask relevant questions, offer appropriate responses, and   10   _____
make the presentation sound conversational

—Ability to be sufficiently demanding of the salesperson by offering at   10   _____
least three objections (A request for more information is not considered
an objection. No objections—0 points, 1 objection—3 points, 2
objections—6 points, and 3 or more objections—10 points.)

                                                    Total   20 pts.   _____

TELEPHONE PROSPECTING

Objectives of Telephone Prospecting

In Chapter 4 we discussed the benefits of using the telephone to schedule appointments. A discussion of the structure and specific content of the telephone call was postponed until this chapter, because knowledge of the concepts discussed in the Approach, Securing Desire, Handling Objections, and Closing the Sale chapters is necessary to understand what to say during the call. This chapter will provide the information you need to complete your Planning Guide for the telephone call to secure an appointment.

The purpose of the telephone call is to secure the appointment. It is not to discuss numerous features and benefits, in an effort to convince the prospect to buy. You are not going to Close the Sale on the telephone. Provide as little information as possible and then request the appointment.

Precall Planning

A great deal of preparation and planning must be done before you actually start dialing the telephone. A list of potential prospects must be developed, including full names, addresses, and telephone numbers. Do some preliminary qualifying. Try to find out who the decision maker is, if he or she has a potential need for your product, whether he or she can buy sufficient quantities to make a face-to-face sales call profitable, and whether the firm has the financial resources to pay for the purchase. Qualifying information can be secured from library sources, other customers and prospects, and a secretary or other personnel at the prospect's firm. Additional qualifying will take place during the face-to-face meeting with the prospect.

Once preliminary qualifying has been completed, additional preparation is necessary to ensure the telephone call will be successful. You may wish to send letters of introduction, such as the one on page 22 for Fusion. What you plan to say during the call must be determined, including how you will Handle Objections. The Planning Guide that follows will help you with this activity. In an actual business setting, it is recommended that a script be written and used to practice the telephone presentation. However, an outline should be used during the actual calls, so your delivery sounds conversational.

You should gather materials you will need during the calls, including an appointment calendar, so you know when you are available for appointments, a pad of paper and pencil to make notes; and the list of potential prospects. Before you start dialing the telephone, you must get "warmed up"; prepare yourself mentally and emotionally. Practice your delivery of the telephone presentation several times out loud. Be aware of your rate of speech, volume, and enunciation. And finally, identify a specific day and time each week for this important activity. Isolate yourself from the noise and confusion of the office. Telephone prospecting requires intense concentration. Spend a minimum of one to two hours each session. After the first few calls, you will find yourself gaining momentum, which increases your closing rate.

Getting through the Gatekeeper

Gatekeepers are typically secretaries and receptionists, who are responsible for screening personal visits and telephone calls, to ensure prospects speak only to salespeople with something of interest. Sometimes it is more difficult to get through the gatekeeper than to convince prospects to grant you an appointment. While the salesperson-prospect dialogue you will develop later in this chapter assumes you have convinced the gatekeeper to allow you to talk to the prospect, it is important to be aware of strategies to get by the gatekeeper. Use these methods only if you encounter resistance:

1. State the general benefit for your product or service to convince him or her it is important for you to talk to the prospect.

2. If you sent the prospect a letter, refer to it. (e.g., "I'm calling to discuss an important letter I sent to Mrs. Gerts.")

3. If you are making a long-distance call, mention it. (e.g., "This is Terry Stiner calling long-distance from Chicago.")

4. Call before or after normal business hours when the gatekeeper is not at his or her desk.

If the prospect is unavailable when you call, find out when he or she is usually available and call back at that time. Be persistent. Do not take "no" for an answer. Consider using a combination of these techniques if you encounter an uncooperative gatekeeper.

Steps in the Telephone Call

Many of the steps in a telephone call to secure an appointment are very similar to steps in the Approach, Handling Objections, and Closing the Sale sections that you have already studied. The main difference is that the telephone call should not exceed two minutes, while a face-to-face sales presentation would be much longer. The following are the steps you should use for your telephone call.

Step 1. Introduce Yourself and Your Company

A telephone call is an intrusion on the prospect's normal routine, so it is imperative that the first 30 seconds be well planned and delivered. When the prospect answers the telephone, he or she wants to know who is calling, why you are calling, and what you want.

Begin the introduction by stating the prospect's name as a question. Make sure you pronounce the name correctly. Pause momentarily so the prospect can respond affirmatively. Then state your first and last name and company name slowly and clearly. Pause for a moment so the prospect can mentally catch up by asking "How are you today?" Speak enthusiastically and in a friendly manner. Smile throughout the telephone call, even though the prospect cannot see you. A smile will change the tone of your delivery and improve the chances of getting the appointment. An introduction might sound like this:

"Mrs. Gerts? (pause) My name is Terry Stiner from ABC Supply Company. How are you today?"

Step 2. Establish a Rapport

When establishing a rapport during a face-to-face sales call, you can spend a minute or two or even longer. During a telephone call, however, you have less time. You should not spend more than five or ten seconds; just long enough to establish common ground between you and the prospect. The following are eight methods to consider. Choose one that seems the most appropriate for what you are selling.

1. *Third party referral, such as from a satisfied customer*—"Sue Walton at Apex Distributing suggested I call you concerning our (product or service)."

2. *Letter sent by the salesperson*—"Last Wednesday I sent you a letter concerning . . . Do you remember seeing it, Mr. Johnson?" If the prospect responds "no," he or she either does not remember receiving it or you are receiving a brush-off. Provide a reason why he or she may not have received it and continue your presentation. An example of a letter to secure an appointment for Jeff Dykehouse, who is selling Fusion, is on page 22.

3. *Written or telephone inquiry from the prospect*—"Mrs. Martin, I'm calling about the inquiry you sent us recently about (product or service)?"

4. *Current prospect's advertising*—"I saw your ad in Sunday's newspaper for the house you are selling on your own, Mr. Quinn."

5. *Current salesperson's advertising*—"By any chance did you see our advertisement in this month's *Engineering World* magazine?" If you get a "no" response, continue your presentation anyway.

6. *Common problem in the prospect's industry*—"Many companies today are experiencing skyrocketing medical insurance costs. Has your company had the same experience, Ms. Ashby?"

7. *Endorsement from a recognized authority in the prospect's industry*—"Mr. Gordon, by any chance did you read in *Sports Illustrated* that Andre Agasse recently agreed to endorse our tennis racquet?"

8. *Personal situation*—"I read in the newspaper you were promoted to Vice-President of Human Resources at Herkner Corporation, Mrs. Jenkins. Congratulations."

Step 3. State Your Purpose and General Benefit

The purpose of this step is to stir the prospect's interest and explain how he or she will benefit from granting you an appointment. Review the discussion on the general benefit in the Approach section of the presentation on pages 31 through 33. Use the same general benefit as in your Approach. You may have to shorten it and change the wording slightly so it flows naturally from Step 2 in this section. Do not explain too much, just explain enough to create interest and a desire to meet with you to learn more about your product or service. Begin the statement as follows:

> "We offer . . . (state the type of product or service you sell). I'm calling to see when we could get together to explain how . . . (state your general benefit)."

Step 4. Close—Ask for an Appointment and Confirm the Details

Request the appointment by providing a series of choices of days and times to meet. Consider the dialogue that follows:

SALESPERSON: (Ask for an appointment.) Are mornings or afternoons best for you, Mrs. Gerts? (Anticipate a brush-off.)

PROSPECT: I guess mornings.

SALESPERSON: Would next Tuesday or Wednesday morning be more convenient?

PROSPECT: Let's make it 9 A.M. on Tuesday.

SALESPERSON: (Confirm the details.) That's great. I'll be there at 9 A.M. next Tuesday. And you're located at 2122 State Street, right?

PROSPECT: Yes. The main entrance and reception area are on the east side of the building.

Step 5. Anticipate Brush-offs

When you request an appointment, you can expect to meet resistance. Since the prospect knows very little about what you sell, the resistance is typically a brush-off and not a valid objection. Attempt to handle the brush-off briefly by providing a cushion, then refer back to your general benefit. The following are some typical brush-offs and ways you might handle them, if you were selling a sales training workshop to a sales manager. The parenthetical information is related to the general benefit.

Prospect's Brush-off	Salesperson's Response
"Mail some information to me about your workshop."	"Our brochure is very general in nature, Mr. Court. It doesn't relate to your specific situation. I could explain much better how (your company will increase its sales and profits) if I met with you in person."
"I'm not interested in a workshop."	"That's only natural, Mr. Court. But I assume your mind isn't closed to proven methods that will (increase your sales and profits)."
"I'm too busy right now."	"Most people in your position are busy, Mr. Court. That is why I'm calling. I wanted to find a convenient time to explain how we can (help you increase your sales and profits)."
"I can't afford any sales training right now.	"Perhaps you can't afford it because (your sales are down). That is exactly why I'm calling, Mr. Court. When we meet I can explain how (the workshop will provide an immediate boost in sales)."
"We *don't need* your workshop."	"You are definitely in a position to know (if your salespeople are well trained), Mr. Court. However, the real question is whether you are open to a proven way (to increase your sales and profits)."

After you respond to the brush-off, ask the prospect for the appointment again by offering him or her a choice between two days, dates, or times, and confirm the details.

Step 6. Thank the Prospect and Terminate the Call

Once the appointment has been secured, many salespeople make the serious error of providing additional features and benefits. These may raise objections, which cannot be resolved, resulting in losing the appointment. The objective of the telephone call is to secure the appointment, so once you have the appointment, thank the prospect and terminate the call.

> "I look forward to meeting you next Tuesday, at 1 P.M. Mrs. Gerts."

Many salespeople send letters to prospects to confirm the day and time of appointments. This helps ensure the prospects will be available when the salesperson arrives for the appointment.

Vocal Expression

It is much easier to secure a commitment from someone in person than on the telephone. When meeting a prospect face-to-face, you have an opportunity to use nonverbal communication, visual aids, and demonstrations. During a telephone call, you have to rely heavily on vocal expression. Your normal conversational voice may or may not be appropriate for telephone communications. You may have to develop a special voice to get prospects' attention and make them listen. Vocal expression involves your rate of speech, volume, tone, enunciation, pitch, vocabulary, and active listening.

Rate of speech—If you speak too quickly, you may sound like a high-pressure salesperson. Speaking too slowly will bore the prospect and fail to hold his or her attention. A proper rate is approximately 150 words per minute, which is what many radio and television announcers use. For most people, this is slower than their normal rate. Record yourself while reading a portion of your sales presentation. Adjust your rate of speech if necessary.

Volume—The volume of your voice must be loud enough to be heard, but not so loud it annoys the prospect. Your mouth should be 1 to 1 ½ inches from the receiver. Use the same volume you would use if you were speaking to someone across the table from you.

Tone—The tone of your voice conveys your telephone personality. Your voice should sound warm, not impersonal; enthusiastic, not bored; sincere, not phony; friendly, not pushy; confident, not timid; and caring, not self-centered. Record your delivery of the telephone call and ask others to evaluate it. Although the prospect cannot see you, smile while you speak. Smiling will help improve the tone of your delivery.

Enunciation—Enunciation involves speaking clearly and understandably. Do not run words together, omit word endings such as "ing," or leave out consonants.

Pitch—If your natural voice is high-pitched, lower it a notch for your telephone delivery. A deeper-sounding voice has a soothing effect and is reassuring. Vary your pitch rather than using a monotone. Good posture while speaking on the telephone will also improve pitch. Holding the telephone on your shoulder or sitting in a slouched position interferes with proper delivery.

Vocabulary—Your delivery *must* sound conversational, so use common words. Avoid technical terms and trade jargon. Incorporate power and action words into the presentation and use the prospect's name.

Active Listening—Indicate you are interested in what the prospect says by using responses like "I see," "uh huh," and "yes."

Example of Telephone Prospecting

The following is an example of the telephone call to secure an appointment for Jeff Dykehouse, who is selling Fusion. He is calling Penny Taylor at Taylor Sports, Inc. It is assumed the prospect was qualified during the Preapproach. She was sent the letter on page 22 before the telephone call.

PLANNING GUIDE—FUSION TELEPHONE PROSPECTING

Salesperson-Prospect Dialogue

Step 1. Introduce yourself and company

SALESPERSON: *(Smile! Speak enthusiastically!) Ms. Taylor?*

PROSPECT: *Yes.*

SALESPERSON: *My name is Jeff Dykehouse from Brooks Shoe, Inc. How are you today?*

PROSPECT: *Pretty good.*

Step 2. Establish a rapport

SALESPERSON: *Last Monday, I sent you a letter concerning our exciting new running shoe, called Fusion. Do you remember seeing it?*

PROSPECT: *Yes*

Step 3. State your purpose and general benefit

SALESPERSON: *You'll recall that in the letter I mentioned Fusion has a new patented feature, which will dramatically improve the running performance of your customers while reducing injuries.*

I'm calling to see when we can get together to discuss how Fusion will increase your athletic shoe sales and profits.

Step 4. Close—Ask for an appointment and confirm the details

SALESPERSON: *Ms. Taylor, are mornings or afternoons best for you?*

SALESPERSON: *(After brush-off) Would next Tuesday or Wednesday morning be more convenient for you?*

PROSPECT: *I guess I could meet with you on Wednesday at 10:30.*

SALESPERSON: *Great! Your office is located at 2122 Main Street, right?*

PROSPECT: *Yes. That's right.*

(Proceed to Step 6.)

PLANNING GUIDE—FUSION TELEPHONE PROSPECTING *(continued)*

Salesperson-Prospect Dialogue

Step 5. Anticipate brush-offs

   Brush-off 1

PROSPECT: *We don't need any more running shoes right now.*

   Response

SALESPERSON: *You are definitely in a position to know if you need new products, Ms. Taylor. However, the real question is whether you are open to a product that is a true breakthrough in running shoe technology—one your customers will love, and one that will provide more profits for your store.*

(Return to Step 4. Attempt to close again.)

   Brush-off 2

PROSPECT: *I'm too busy right now.*

   Response

SALESPERSON: *Most people in your position are busy, Ms. Taylor. That's why I'm calling. I wanted to find a convenient time to explain how we can help you increase your athletic shoe sales and profits.*

(Return to Step 4. Attempt to close again.)

Step 6. Thank the prospect and terminate the call

SALESPERSON: *I look forward to meeting you next Wednesday at 10:30, Ms. Taylor.*

Preparing to Role Play

Planning Guide Form—Telephone Prospecting

Complete the following Planning Guide for your telephone call. Use one of the methods discussed on page 121 to establish a rapport. Also, choose two brush-offs similar to the ones discussed on page 122 and develop appropriate responses for each. Provide a complete dialogue of what you and the prospect say. Complete the form neatly using number 2 pencil, so it can be changed and photocopied. Study the rating form on page 131 to make sure you have not forgotten anything.

PLANNING GUIDE—FUSION TELEPHONE PROSPECTING

Salesperson-Prospect Dialogue

Refer to the example of the completed Planning Guide on page 125 and 126.

Step 1. Introduce yourself and your company *(Fill out this form neatly in number 2 pencil. Write small. See page 120 and 121.)*

Step 2. Establish a rapport *(Use one of the methods discussed on page 121.)*

Step 3. State your purpose and general benefit (See page 121.)

Step 4. Close—Ask for an appointment and confirm the details (See page 122.) *(PROSPECT: Offer one brush-off after the salesperson requests an appointment.)*

(Proceed to Step 6 on the next page.)

PLANNING GUIDE—FUSION TELEPHONE PROSPECTING *(continued)*

Salesperson-Prospect Dialogue

Step 5. Anticipate brush-offs *(Choose two brush-offs on page 122. Adapt them for your product or service.)*

Brush-off 1

Response

(Return to Step 4. Attempt to close again.)

Brush-off 2

Response

(Return to Step 4. Attempt to close again.)

Step 6. Thank the prospect and terminate the call *(See page 123.)*

How the Role Play Will Be Conducted

Your sales manager may have you role play the telephone call during a training session. If not, you should role play it on your own or with two people. The prospect should offer one of the brush-offs in the Planning Guide. Respond to the brush-off and try to close again. Pay close attention to your delivery, including rate of speech, volume, tone, enunciation, pitch, and active listening. The coach can complete the rating form on page 131. During the role play, the salesperson and prospect should be seated back-to-back to eliminate any exchanges of non-verbal communications.

Materials Needed to Role Play the Telephone Call

You will need your Setting the Scene Form on page 39, Planning Guide, a photocopy of the Planning Guide for the prospect, Telephone Prospecting Rating Form, and *RPPS* manual. If you do not have access to a photocopy machine, make a typewritten or handwritten copy of the complete salesperson-prospect dialogue, including the listing of the steps.

Telephone Prospecting Rating Form (25 Points)

Salesperson's Company: _____   Hour: _____

Product/Service: _____   Salesperson's Name: _____

Prospect's Company: _____	Possible Score	Actual Score		
		Record Scores of Three Role Plays		
—Ability to introduce yourself and establish a rapport	2	_____	_____	_____
—Ability to state your purpose and general benefit	4	_____	_____	_____
—Ability to handle a brush-off	4	_____	_____	_____
—Ability to ask for an appointment by offering a choice of dates and times	4	_____	_____	_____
—Ability to confirm the details of the appointment, thank the prospect, and terminate the call	2	_____	_____	_____
—Ability to use proper telephone communications techniques, including	4	_____	_____	_____
—Ability to sound conversational	5	_____	_____	_____
Total	25 pts.	_____	_____	_____

—Ability to use proper telephone communications techniques, including

    —rate of speech   —pitch
    —volume   —vocabulary
    —tone   —active listening
    —enunciation

Coach's notes and comments: